# An Introduction to Revelation

# The Continuum Biblical Studies Series

SERIES EDITOR: STEVE MOYISE

The Continuum Biblical Studies Series is aimed at those taking a course of biblical studies. Developed for the use of those embarking on theological and ministerial education, it is equally helpful in local church situations, and for lay people confused by apparently conflicting approaches to the Scriptures.

Students of biblical studies today will encounter a diversity of interpretive positions. Their teachers will – inevitably – lean towards some positions of preference to others. This series offers an integrated approach to the Bible which recognizes this diversity, but helps readers to understand it, and to work towards some kind of unity within it.

This is an ecumenical series, written by Roman Catholics and Protestants. The writers are all professionally engaged in the teaching of biblical studies in theological and ministerial education. The books are the product of that experience, and it is the intention of the editor, Dr Steve Moyise, that their contents should be tested on this exacting audience.

# An Introduction
# to Revelation

GILBERT DESROSIERS

**CONTINUUM**
London and New York

9

**Continuum**
Wellington House, 125 Strand, London WC2R 0BB
370 Lexington Avenue, New York, NY 10017-6503

© 2000 Gilbert Desrosiers

The Scripture quotations contained herein are from the New Revised Standard
Version Bible, copyright © 1989 by the Division of Christian Education of the
National Council of the Churches of Christ in the USA, and are used by
permission. All rights reserved.

First published 2000

**British Library Cataloguing-in-Publication Data.**
A catalogue record for this book is available from the British Library.

ISBN 0-8264-5002-4

Typeset by BookEns Ltd, Royston, Herts
Printed and bound in Great Britain by Biddles Ltd
*www.biddles.co.uk*

# Contents

# Introduction: Revelation in the News

## Heaven's Gate, Branch Davidians, Solar Temple and the book of Revelation

The events surrounding The Branch Davidians' fiery end at Waco, Texas; the simultaneous suicides of the members of the Order of the Solar Temple in Switzerland and Quebec, as well as the Heaven's Gate's deadly 'beam up' of March 1997 at Rancho Santa Fe conjure up dark images and raise puzzling questions. Why would any normal, balanced, human being join such marginal groups often labelled 'Doomsday Cults'? Most answers usually fall short of totally enlightening and comforting us. A close analysis of these three groups has revealed a common thread of apocalyptic symbols and visions weaving a tapestry of nightmarish images and occult longings. Each group had incorporated, into its various ideologies and behaviours, elements taken from the book of Revelation.

David Koresh, in his delusion of grandeur, considered himself to be the reincarnation of Lenin and Jesus Christ (nice combination!). His overriding desire was to ignite the fires of Armageddon in order to bring about his own parousia as the Son of Man. The Solar Temple members, during their secret ceremonies reminiscent of the Knight Templars, wore 'red and gold medallions ... which bore an inscription invoking the Four Horsemen of the Apocalypse' (Cook, 1995, p. 4). In turn, Bonnie Nettles and Marshall Applewhite, twin founders and leaders of the Heaven's Gate cult, saw themselves as the 'two witnesses' of Revelation 11.

These events which stunned North American and European society have brought about a renewed call for guidelines in the interpretation of books such as the Revelation of John. The arrival of the new millennium has transformed this call into an urgency which cannot be ignored without dire consequences. As Umberto Eco underlined in his exchange with Carlo Cardinal Martini of Milan, 'The Book of

Revelation can be read as a promise, but also as the announcement of an end; in this sense it is constantly being rewritten during this time of waiting for the year 2000, even by those who have never read it' (Eco and Martini, 1997, p. 381). A question then arises, 'How does one study such a book?'

## Apocalypse and millennium fever

As witnessed throughout the ages, the interpretation of the book of Revelation has often resulted in deadly scenarios being enacted. Its dark images of persecution, battles, plagues and destruction have fed the minds of countless individuals who saw in its pages the tortured signs of the imminent consummation of history. The power of its visions has given Western civilization some of its most admired paintings and works of literature. Its complex symbols and seemingly anti-Christian values have baffled even the best among biblical interpreters. This awe-inspiring book has also become the repository of truth for believers and non-believers who search for meaning and comfort in the face of unexplainable catastrophes.

The use and abuse of the book of Revelation has been quite remarkable in times of great danger and periods leading to a change of eras. The third millennium has fed a renewed desire to decipher the message which lies at the heart of Revelation. For Christians, this latent fear of facing a new millennium has frequently been linked to the concept of an apocalypse, a final confrontation between the forces of Good and Evil which would culminate in the Second Coming of Christ and the establishment of his eternal kingdom. This apocalypse has been described in terms and images pooled directly from the pages of the book of Revelation whose very first word *apocalypsis* can be translated either as 'revelation' or 'apocalypse'. What is one to make of such affirmations? Is Revelation a blueprint of the end of the world? Is Revelation a survival guide to the final tribulation? Should it be discarded from the Christian library for, as Martin Luther once stated, 'not teaching Christ'. How is one to use such a book? Can a believer find any Christian sustenance in a document filled with blood, beasts and gore?

## The need for hermeneutics

The act of reading has always had as its corollary, the act of interpretation; making sense of what has just been read. Any text 'conveys to us a certain initial understanding of its meaning. The task of interpretation is to discuss and elaborate this initial understanding and if necessary to correct it, in order that the text itself may speak to us' (WCC, 1980, p. 36). A staple of modern hermeneutics is the view that reading, decoding, and understanding is a complex phenomenon fraught with internal and external difficulties.

Hermeneutics refers to a theory of interpretation or to the different methodologies used to practise interpretation. Hermeneutics is not in itself a modern phenomenon. We can go back to the first Christian communities and find ways of reading a text which involved a specific methodology. The communities of Alexandria in Egypt and Antioch in Syria were prime examples of this. The Alexandrians became well known for their use of the allegorical method. Origen (*c.* 185–*c.* 254) remains the ultimate representative of that school of Christian hermeneutics. On the other hand, the school of Antioch was characterized by its literal approach to the biblical text, in manifest opposition to the Alexandrians. Both of these methods allowed one to say something about how the book of Revelation was to be interpreted.

Christian hermeneutics has come a long way since the time of these two schools of thought. Nonetheless, its basic goal is still to find the most adequate method for interpreting biblical texts. The question of interpretation has been brought to the fore once more, in part due to the catastrophes linked to misinterpretations of writings like the book of Revelation. How is one to decide that a particular reading is the correct one? What are the textual clues leading one to a valid interpretation of a given book of the Bible? Is the meaning of a text objective or subjective? Is the meaning to be found in the text itself, the author's intent, in the act of reading, or in an interplay between text and reader? These questions have been and are still hotly debated. One's answers will determine, or at least influence, the choice of an interpretive method.

The question also arises as to how anyone can evaluate the results of others' readings. This is due mostly to the fact that ultimately, interpretation, taking ownership of a text, is an act of re-creation similar to a Mozart concerto being in some way re-created as it is interpreted by the various musicians who perform it. How am I to critique anyone's 're-creation' of Revelation? What can help one assess the validity of a given interpretation? Is it at all possible?

However, there is no need to panic and jump to the conclusion that every interpretation is the sole result of communal or individual subjectivity. Interpretation of any concerto would not exist if the concerto was not already open to this possibility. This musical work remains the condition of its interpretation. The Bible could not be interpreted and actualized if it were not already in itself the condition and possibility of all interpretations. Because of its status as historical and living, the Word of God screams out to be interpreted. To interpret is to release the power and energy of the Word in an act of faithful re-creation.

For Christian believers who approach the Bible in order to study it faithfully, another factor comes into consideration, the role of the Spirit of God as hermeneutical guide, as ultimate representative of the meaning of Scriptures. The Spirit of God, alive and active in the believer, remains the ultimate subjective side of Scriptures, moving the believer towards a meaningful study and understanding of the biblical message. The Word of God, objectively inscribed in Scriptures requires a subjective legitimization, the Spirit. Only the Spirit will ensure a full capacity to listen to the Word. Nonetheless, we do not find ourselves with a constant dichotomy of Scriptures on one side and the Spirit on the other. The Spirit inhabits Scriptures in active waiting of an interpreter whom it has itself already summoned to the study of the Word.

This then brings us to ask: What is the knowledge needed in order to be able to properly access, assess, and use the huge amount of information available on any biblical text, including Revelation? What is needed in order to study this powerful piece of literature and be able to understand and critique other's readings and interpretations? This 'Introduction to Revelation' will attempt to answer these questions.

In the following pages, you will be presented with the basic tools and information required in order to be able to access and assess the wide variety of monographs, commentaries, and periodical articles relating to the book of Revelation. Revelation being a complex piece of literature, you might find that to read and study it in a serious, responsible manner might seem like a daunting task. It is. Very few books of the Bible have caused as many rifts between biblical commentators and among Christian communities as Revelation has in the past nineteen centuries. You will find yourself having to choose and take a stand on many issues. This may seem intimidating, but it is the inevitable result of the human condition expressed in the acts of reading and interpreting.

This *Introduction* does not aim at presenting a verse-by-verse commentary of Revelation, nor does it intend to address all the technical issues involved in the study of this book. The goal is first to offer a map which will help the beginning student find his/her way through the maze of commentaries and articles which have been written on the book of Revelation. Next, it will strive to help the reader/student identify where the different positions expounded by various commentators come from. Lastly, it should enable the reader to grasp the main issues and basic questions that need to be addressed when studying the Apocalypse. Our wish is that the information contained in this basic introduction will nurture a confidence and a curiosity in the reader which will translate into a desire to experience John of Patmos' vision and be among those recipients of God's blessing:

> Blessed is the one who reads aloud the words of the prophecy, and blessed are those who hear and who keep what is written in it; for the time is near. (Rev 1.3)

# 1

## Lifting the Veil on Revelation

Interpreting the Bible entails, first of all, a recognition of its claim of being the Word of God revealed in history through a series of human communicators. This dual aspect of biblical literature, divine and human, highlights how the acceptance or denial of this basic claim can influence any reading and interpretation of Scriptures. How can Revelation be considered 'Word of God'? What was the role of the writer John in the whole process? Is Revelation only human literature? Since John claimed that the medium of this heaven–earth communication was visions, more needs to be said concerning the nature and function of this phenomenon.

### Revelation as divine communication

The book of Revelation presents itself as a direct communication from God to one of his servants, John: 'The revelation of Jesus Christ, which God gave him to show his servants what must soon take place; he made it known by sending his angel to his servant John …' (Rev. 1.1). This clear statement of the divine origin of Revelation's message forces the interpreter to take a stand: accept or deny this claim to otherworldly status. Interpreters are divided on this issue. Most scholars who follow the historical-critical method, with its full rationalist background, have a tendency to deny divine authority to the text in order to preserve their freedom of inquiry and interpretation. Most schools of thought influenced by the Enlightenment follow this line of thought.

Most confessional scholars, linked to some denominational creed or statement of faith, accept the divine prerogative claimed by the text and keep this as the foundation of all interpretation. Roman Catholic, Orthodox and Evangelical scholars are good examples of this basic stance toward the interpretation of Revelation. This acceptance of John's Apocalypse as divine communication finds expression in the theory of biblical inspiration and its corollary, biblical inerrancy.

A basic belief found in all Christian denominations is that Holy Scriptures were inspired by God. Even though it is part of every Christian denomination's beliefs, divine inspiration is not interpreted by all in the same way. The various definitions move from complete mechanical inspiration, where God is seen as having dictated each and every word of Scriptures directly to each biblical writer, to free inspiration where God is seen as having influenced the religious, moral message found in Scriptures in some way or another, with the onus being on the human writer. One's location on this divine inspiration spectrum gives interpretive results a specific shade and colour. It is thus important to realize that to view Revelation as an example of divine communication is to accept from the start the claims presented by the text itself.

The theory of divine inspiration is often accompanied by an important corollary: biblical inerrancy. Biblical inerrancy stipulates that no error is to be found in the biblical text, whether the information be historical or moral. This is a logical development of the doctrine of inspiration. If the Bible is the Word of God, then it cannot contain any error since God cannot make any mistakes. The advancement of science has ignited many heated debates concerning the validity of this belief.

Various forms of mitigated biblical inerrancy are found in several Christian denominations. Critical scholars who isolate themselves from specific denominational faith statements usually deny the theory of biblical inerrancy and put emphasis on the possibility of error coming from the original writers or later copyists. When applied to the book of Revelation, inerrancy is sailing in rough waters. How is inerrancy to be applied to a book which abounds with symbols?

To view Revelation as divine communication is to emphasize first of all that its primary author is God himself. It is to acknowledge the text's claim as possessing divine authority. This then will influence the way in which we study and interpret this book. Since we cannot fathom the will of God, our interpretations of Revelation will always be partial and incomplete. But what of the original channel of this communication? What about the human writer?

## Revelation as human communication

The book of Revelation, like all books of the Bible, is the result in part of human activity. How much human activity depends on one's view of the divine inspiration of Scriptures. For those who believe in a totally mechanistic view of inspiration, the human writer was nothing but a keyboard used by God to put text to parchment. The human writer had no say in the choice of words used or anything else for that matter. Human activity is considered as having been extremely minimal.

At the other end of the spectrum, we find those who believe that the book of Revelation was nothing but the result of human activity. These interpreters consider all aspects of the book as being the end product of a series of human decisions. Divine influence is ignored or reduced to an insignificant part of the whole process. Consequently, this allows the interpreter to approach the text using all the tools of historical and literary criticism. The emphasis on the human factor opens the book up to a series of questions which will greatly impact on its interpretation.

First, this emphasis allows one to question in detail the identity and intention of the human author behind the text of Revelation. Who was this author, this man who called himself John? What was his social background? Why did he decide to write this book? What was his purpose? Who was he writing to? Second, it begs the question of the literary nature of the book of Revelation. What type of writing does it represent? Is it to be read as an edifying tale or as predictive prophecy? Third, affirming the human side of Revelation lets one question the value of this writing for today's Christians. What are we to do with this book? Does it hold any value for Christians facing the beginning of the third millennium?

## From earth to heaven and back: the dynamics of visions

The study of the interaction between the human and the divine in the communication process takes on great significance when applied to the book of Revelation. This is due to the presence of the expression 'in the Spirit', *en pneumati*, which occurs in Revelation at 1.10; 4.2; 17.3; and 21.10. This expression, found mainly in the vision reports of the prophet Ezekiel, 'is best understood as a technical term for the visionary's experience of "rapture" by the Spirit ... denoting both the visionary experience as such and the Spirit's authorship of it' (Bauckham, 1993a, p. 152). This Spirit took hold of the visionary and brought about a form of ecstasy/trance which shut down the visionary's senses while opening up his inner eye to a higher level of reality. The seer's body was shocked into inactivity while his mind was flooded with images and sounds. How did these visions take place? What were the psychological processes behind such phenomena? How could the information received through these visions be expressed in a way that would make them understandable to others? How did the seer perceive the visions?

Since most of the information imparted to John is claimed as having come through visions, every interpreter of Revelation will have to make sense of the seer's experience. Was there anything 'objective' to these visions? Did John actually see what he said he saw? If so, how can one put into words things which by their very nature are almost ineffable and elude propositional language? How is the reader to interpret these revelations – as a realistic, 'photographically precise image' (Roloff, 1993, p. 13) or an impressionist canvas?

Some interpreters define the visions as being 'objective' meaning that there was something out there which John saw and faithfully described. Others consider these same visions to have been 'subjective': literary artifices concocted entirely by John as a way of expressing his message. Still others locate themselves midway between the objective and the subjective interpretation of the visions. They consider the visionary experience as being genuine. John did see something which he did not invent and which he perceived while in a trance-like state. At the same time, these interpreters stress that when it came time to write these visions down, John used his literary and religious tradition: 'as a literary and theological artist, he consciously selects the language he uses to portray the vision' (Boring, 1989, p. 83). All this was done in order to convey the message John perceived as central to the visions' meaning.

Because of their prophetic nature, these visions could not remain John's sole property, but were to be written down and circulated. The task of communicating such things in a written format is problematic since it entails enabling the hearer/reader to relive what John experienced first hand. What kind of language could allow one to accomplish this complex task: propositional or symbolic? Could divine communication be faithfully conveyed by human words? The answer to this last question will markedly define one's stand toward the nature and value of John's visions as well as the way he reported them.

# 2

## The Story

The minimal use of Revelation in Christian lectionaries and the overemphasis put on the interpretation of the millennium in Revelation 20 have led the majority of Christians to bypass a fundamental aspect of Revelation: its story. Readers who face the text of Revelation in a continuous translation, without chapter and verse division, are quickly caught up in the narrative which unfolds before their eyes. In order to analyse specific elements of this work, it is important first to read the story from beginning to end and realize that it is united by narrative elements such as characters, plot and setting.

As with the Gospels and Paul's letters, Revelation was originally meant to be read aloud, probably in one sitting, during prayer assemblies or eucharistic gatherings. The extremely limited use of Revelation in the various Christian lectionaries does not offer today's hearers the capacity to recognize the unity and movement of the story. Revelation was meant to be experienced as a whole so that the hearers could, in some way, relive the visionary experience of the seer of Patmos. In order to bring this experience to the fore, we will now turn our attention to the different narrative elements found in Revelation and conclude with the presentation of an outline for the book. At this time, it is recommended that the reader tackles the task of reading Revelation in one or two sittings, paying special attention to characters, plot, and setting. This would probably facilitate the comprehension of the following presentation.

### The actors

When reading the book of Revelation, one cannot but be amazed at the sheer number and diversity of characters encountered throughout the story. Revelation is replete with characters belonging to different worlds, human and divine, as well as a menagerie of strange creatures, bestial and angelic. This variety, as well as sheer quantity, often leaves the reader bewildered, trying to remember the role(s) each character has been playing. The attributes of these characters are closely linked to the nature of John's visionary experience, which brought along an extensive use of symbols.

The characters found in Revelation do not all have the same importance in the development of the story. As with all plays or feature films, we find major and minor characters, as well as cameo appearances by well-known figures. We will now list these characters, in a non-exhaustive way, and highlight some of their peculiar features, if any. It is to be further noticed that the definition of character used for this chapter includes all beings or objects which play an active or passive role in the unfolding of the story line. One could raise objections to having inanimate objects considered characters instead of props. However, due to the visionary and highly symbolic aspects of Revelation, the notion of character must become all-encompassing. The following presentation of the characters does not follow the story line, but rather focuses on the importance given to each of these in the story. The more notorious figures of Revelation will be presented before the lesser-known ones. Some characters do resurface throughout the story under various aliases. For our presentation, the introduction and analysis of a specific charac-ter will include all relevant aliases. It is now time to take a look at some of these.

## The cast of characters

### Jesus Christ
The book of Revelation is presented as a revelation of Jesus Christ. The Greek expression *apocalypsis Iesou Christou* can be understood in two ways: a revelation which is given by Jesus Christ or a revelation which talks about Jesus Christ. Interpreters have been divided on this subject. If we look at it from a narrative point of view, we realize that Jesus Christ is the main character, or protagonist, of Revelation. His presence is highlighted from the start of the book all the way to the end. The figure of Christ includes many aliases. They are the following:

- One like the Son of Man (1.13; 14.14)
- The slain/yet standing Lamb (6.6; 14.1)
- A male child (12.5)
- The Rider on the white horse (19.11)

### John
John, the seer of Patmos, is not only the one who is addressing the seven churches and who presents himself as the author of the book of

Revelation, but he is simultaneously an actor in the visionary drama which unfolds. John thus acts both as a narrator and a character. A quick look at the nature of a narrator and the role he/she plays in the story-telling process will help us get a better understanding of the function John plays in Revelation. A narrator is a creation of a specific author. The narrator is a device used by the writer to tell his story and is rarely identical with the author, even if sometimes they have a lot in common.

There exist different levels of narration. At the outer level of narration, we encounter 'the one who reads aloud the words of the prophecy'. We do not know who this person was because it would have changed from one public reading to the next. The next level of narration is represented by John, the individual who sees the vision. But, as he sees the vision and reports it, he also acts as a character. The third level of narration happens when a pure character (in contrast to John who is writer/character) narrates the action. This happens when the figure of the One like the Son of Man narrates to John the seven letters to the churches of Asia. The narrator embodies values which can be either identical or different from those of the author. The narrator, depending on the level of narration, also possesses a certain knowledge which can allow him/her to evaluate or pass judgement on some of the characters or events found in the story.

### The seven churches
The seven churches named and addressed in the first three chapters of Revelation are explicit and implicit characters. They are explicitly involved in those first three chapters but remain in the background for the remainder of the book. It is to be remembered that when John was presenting his visionary experience, it was first for the benefit of these seven churches. These seven communities represented seven churches located today in Turkey.

### Satan
The main antagonist in the book of Revelation is the character of the Devil, Satan, the Great Dragon. Even if he is not always in the foreground, many of the actions taking place derive from his plan and influence. Much of the work of this character is done in the background until he appears on the scene as the Great Red Dragon, the serpent (12.3ff.).

### One seated on the throne
God is represented in Revelation in a way which is very similar to the throne vision found in Isaiah 6.1 and Ezekiel 1.26–28. God himself was

not described directly, only his throne, his outward manifestation. The throne of God represented his presence. This way of indirectly describing the deity was very ancient, going back to the time of the Babylonian and Canaanite religions. The storm-god Baal, or his father El, would often be represented by a bull. The bull itself was not Baal, nor El, but his pedestal, his footstool. Instead of trying to describe the unfathomable being of God, most visionaries would concentrate on the description of the throne on which he was sitting.

### The heavenly entourage

When John is taken to heaven to behold his vision, we encounter characters which seem to represent God's royal court. These are the four beings and the twenty-four elders. The four beings (4.6, 8; 5.6, 8, 14; 6.1, 6; 7.11; 14.3; 15.7; 19.4) are reminiscent of visions found in Ezekiel 1.5ff. and Isaiah 6.2–3. The origin of these fantastic creatures is most likely to be found in Babylonian mythology. The twenty-four elders (4.4, 10; 5.8; 11.16; 19.4) play a large role in the recurring heavenly liturgy which punctuates the story. The image might have originated from the institution of court advisors found in many cultures.

### Angels

These inhabitants of the heavenly realm, who act as intermediaries between God and human beings, are ever present in the book of Revelation. By the time the Apocalypse of John was written Judaism had acquired a somewhat systematized angelology (study of the nature and role of angels). Its influence pervades the book of Revelation. The angels are mostly minor characters in relation to Revelation's plot, but the sheer number of scenes and actions in which they are involved bestows on them a special status. The angels are usually described through their actions: the revelatory angel (1.1), the seven angelic representatives of the seven churches (2.1 – 3.22), the seven angels with the seven trumpets/bowls-plagues (8.2; 15.1, 7), the guiding angel (22.8), the angel of the waters (16.5), etc. Sometimes they are named: Michael, the leader of the angelic army (12.7); Abbadon/Apollyon, the angel of the bottomless pit (9.11). Angels are therefore very much part of Revelation's cast of characters.

### The beasts

As a foil (character who highlights the protagonist by either being a parallel or a contrast) to the Lamb and the four living beings who serve God's throne, we find the characters of the two beasts. The first beast possesses seven heads and ten horns and rises from the sea (13.1). The second beast rises out of the earth. (13.11, foreshadowed in 11.7). It has two horns like a lamb and speaks like a dragon. This character possesses an alias as the false prophet (16.13; 19.20; 20.10). These two bestial characters are very closely linked to that of the Great Dragon. Their interaction emphasizes their close narrative relationship.

## The women

Feminine characters play a considerable role in the book of Revelation. Positive and negative female images are offered, often in direct contrast to one another. The first female image is that of a female prophet in the church at Thyatira whom John derisively calls Jezebel, identifying her with the wife of king Ahab who massacred the prophets of the Lord and was devoured by dogs (1 Kings 16.31 – 2 Kings 9.36). The next female character is the woman clothed with the sun (12.1ff.) who gives birth to a male child and is hunted by the Great Red Dragon. This image has been interpreted in many ways: from the goddess Leto who gives birth to Apollo and is chased by the dragon Python; to Israel, as the bride of the Lord giving birth to the Messiah; to Mary of Nazareth giving birth to Jesus. The next woman is the great whore (17.1). She is described as a prostitute, dressed in purple and scarlet, adorned with jewels and gold, and drunk with the blood of the saints. She is identified by her name: Babylon. She is used as a foil to the last female character of Revelation, the Bride of the Lamb (19.7; 21.2, 9; 22.17), who is identified as the New Jerusalem.

## The Spirit

The Spirit plays an extensive role in Revelation. This role is manifold and diversified. At the start of the book, John finds himself in the spirit on the day of the Lord (1.10). The word 'spirit' in this passage, is not capitalized, contrary to what we find in the verses where the Spirit talks to the churches. This capitalization was probably non-existent in the original Greek text, since until the tenth century many ancient manuscripts were written completely in uncials, letters having all the same size. The capitalization that is found in English translations is mainly due to someone's interpretation. The word 'spirit' with a small case seems to represent John's ecstatic state (as in 1.10; 4.2; 17.3; 21.10) while 'Spirit' capitalized, represents the Spirit of God. The Spirit plays a central role as a communication agent in the 'letters' section of the book (2.1 – 3.22). The seven spirits of God (3.1; 4.5; 5.6) are also present as characters. Their role seems likewise to be that of communication agents sent throughout all the earth.

## The remainder of the cast of characters

The book of Revelation contains a large number of supporting characters. Within the earthly setting we find riders on white, red, black and pale horses; as well as kings, merchants, shipmasters, sailors, followers of the beast, faithful witnesses of the Lord, slaves, rich and poor people. In the heavenly realm we find the souls of the martyrs, an innumerable multitude robed in white, 144,000 sealed ones, and people on thrones. We also encounter a great variety of objects, creatures and places which are personified (given human attributes) and thus can interact at the same level as human characters: an eagle who cries with a loud voice (8.13); a Lamb who leads an army; the earth which opens its mouth (12.16); an altar that responds to God (16.7); the new Jerusalem which acts as a bride (21.9-10); Death and Hades who are punished like all other unbelievers (20.14).

This panoply of major and minor characters bestows on Revelation a kaleidoscopic quality which sometimes can be overpowering for the reader. It is difficult to follow each of the main characters since they often go under a variety of aliases. One is sometimes left asking 'who is who?' It is also to be noticed that although the number of characters involved in Revelation is quite high, they tend to remain static and flat. Static characters do not develop throughout the narrative and flat characters remain basically one-dimensional, thus predictable. All these characters are very closely linked to the next narrative element: the setting.

## The setting

Every story is presented as taking place somewhere, at some time, in a certain cultural/social environment. These locational, chronological, and cultural/social elements are all part of what is called the setting. The physical setting is the actual environment in which the characters act and interact, and where the action takes place. The chronological setting is the time period in which the action is happening. This can be the hour, the day, the year or the era when the story is developing. The cultural/social setting represents the values, principles, customs and behaviours that are normative in the world of the story.

When studying the question of setting, whether physical, chronological or cultural/social, we must first distinguish between the historical setting and the setting of the story. The historical physical setting refers to the actual location occupied by the author of Revelation when writing his narrative. In the case of John, this seems to have been Patmos (Rev 1.9), an island in the Aegean sea. For a narrative analysis of Revelation we must concentrate on the setting of the story world. This means studying the place and time where the events of the story are unfolding.

The physical setting of Revelation is very diversified. John's story takes place in two main environments: earth and heaven. The earthly setting is composed of various locations. The main one is Patmos. This is where the story starts. John is dictating the letters to the seven churches while on the island of Patmos. These same letters offer an evaluation of what is happening in another setting: Asia, more specifically the seven cities of Ephesus, Smyrna, Pergamum, Thyatira, Sardis, Philadelphia and Laodicea. As part of the earthly setting, we also find the whole earth, the four corners of the earth, the sea and the seashore, mount Zion, Armageddon, the wilderness and the river Euphrates. The heavenly setting, on the other hand, includes the throne, the heavenly temple, the altar, the sun, the lake of fire, and the abyss, among others.

The chronological setting is also puzzling. According to the seer John, the whole visionary experience takes place on 'the day of the Lord' (1.10). The whole narrative would thus logically unfold during that one day. However, in the world of the visions, the second narrative level, chronological settings and indications abound. We read of a half-an-hour silence (8.1), of 1260 days (11.3 and 12.6), the days of their ('the two witnesses') prophesying (11.6), three and a half days (11.9, 11), day and night (4.8; 7.15; 12.10; 14.11; 20.10; 21.25). We also read of a thousand-year period (20.2–7). These time markers all seem to imply the presence of alternate chronological settings, leading the reader to wonder when the action is actually taking place.

As stated before, the cultural/social setting represents the values, principles, customs and behaviours which are normative in the story world. However, this cultural/social setting found in the story world is often directly linked to the historical cultural environment in which the real author lived. This means that we must become acutely aware of the historical location of the first-century author known as John and the churches to which he was writing. Our knowledge of first-century Christianity being sometimes incomplete, we might occasionally be stymied by some custom or behaviour described in Revelation.

The cultural setting of Revelation's story world is one made up of contrasts. The attitudes and beliefs accepted as normative by the main characters of the story are clear-cut. In the letters sent to the seven churches, the figure of Christ lays down all the normative elements required of a true believer: patient endurance, steadfastness during persecution, faithfulness until death, love, service, repentance. These values are then illustrated through the use of the various major and minor characters. These same values and behaviours are highlighted by the presence of characters who do not live up to these expectations. An example of that would be the people who listen to the beast and receive its mark, versus the saints who do not. The former are thrown in the lake of fire while the latter sing the song of Moses and of the Lamb.

The richness of Revelation's physical, chronological and cultural settings imbues it with an aura of mystery and ultimate urgency. The time has come, heaven meets earth, and the faithful are vindicated. The link between the characters and the settings will help the action develop and allow the story to reach its resolution. Therefore, the question of plot in Revelation needs to be examined attentively.

## Plot, events, and story

The search for hidden clues, which could allow one to predict the future and anticipate the End, has led many to ignore Revelation's story. This has taken away from the richness of the book and the message it is conveying. The reading experience can be greatly enhanced if the various devices and mechanisms by which all try to 'make sense' of a story are made explicit (Moyise, 1998, pp. 53–67). Of particular importance is the idea of 'plot'. The notion of plot usually refers to '(t)he sequence of events in a story, usually based on a central conflict and having a beginning, middle, and end' (Ryken, 1992, p. 516). A cursory look at Revelation shows that it does contain a beginning, a middle and an end. However, in order to have a plot, the events must stand in a cause–effect relationship to one another; meaning that something happens which triggers something else in return. The example often quoted to illustrate this point is the following: 'The king died and then the queen died.' This would not be considered a plot since the death of the queen is not linked in a cause–effect relationship to the death of the king. In order for this little statement to become a story with a plot, some kind of causal nexus would have to be introduced: 'The king died, and then, out of unending, inconsolable grief, the queen jumped off the castle's tower and died.' We now have a full cause–effect link between the death of the king and that of the queen. We now have a plot. It is to be conceded that, sometimes, the causal link might not be overtly expressed and will require the discernment of the reader in order to be recognized.

A plot is usually built around the principles of unity, coherence and emphasis. If Revelation does possess a plot, we should be able to identify these elements. Most plots are also organized around some form of conflict. This conflict might be physical, moral, spiritual or psychological. The plot will therefore consist in one of these conflicts moving from its inception to its resolution.

In the case of Revelation, the plot conflict is first of all a spiritual one between good and evil. This basic plot conflict is then developed through a character conflict between Christ and the Devil/Satan, ar character conflicts between their respective followers. All of the develop through the events which constitute Revelation's plot.

Readers often take for granted that the events described in a story a presented in chronological order. Sometimes, however, an event will I introduced which breaks the chronological unfolding of the story I throwing the readers back in time or by giving them a glimpse of th future. In order to understand the role played by these tempor displacements, we first have to consider the difference between *sto time* and *discourse time*.

*Story time* is a term which refers to the order of events as they unfold i the story. As an example, when reading the gospels we expect that Jesu will be arrested, tried and executed in that order, because logically this the only way these events would make sense. However, the narrator of th story might intervene to present something which does not fit into th forward chronological flow of the story. We say that such happenings a part of *discourse time*. Discourse time 'refers to the order in which th events are described for the reader by the narrator' (Powell, 1990, p. 36

When story time and discourse time do not match, we are facin something we will call *time distortion*. These time distortions can b divided in two categories, depending on whether they deal with even' which actually happened before or after the event which is now bein described. If the event is in the past, we call this a *flashback*. If the eve being described gives the reader a glimpse into the future of the stor' we call this a *foreshadowing*. The following would be an example of flashback. In Revelation 1, John sees a vision of the risen Christ, whil in Revelation 12.1–2, 5 we read:

> A great portent appeared in heaven: a woman clothed with the sun, with the moon under her feet, and on her head a crown of twelve stars. She was pregnant and was crying out in birth pangs, in the agony of giving birth. And she gave birth to a son, a male child, who is to rule all the nations with a rod of iron. But her child was snatched away and taken to God and to his throne ...

If this vision is related to the birth of the Messiah, we have here a example of a flashback. This event throws us back in time to th moment of Jesus' birth while, in the story, the Dragon is already wagin war against those who hold to the testimony of the resurrected Jesus. I Revelation, we also find scenes which anticipate or describe the futur victory of the saints of God. One example of such foreshadowing i found in Revelation 7.9, 13–14 where we read:

> After this I looked, and there was a great multitude that no one could count, from every nation, from all tribes and peoples and languages,

standing before the throne and before the Lamb, robed in white, with palm branches in their hands. Then one of the elders addressed me, saying, 'Who are these, robed in white, and where have they come from?' I said to him, 'Sir, you are the one that knows.' Then he said to me, 'These are they who have come out of the great ordeal; they have washed their robes and made them white in the blood of the Lamb.'

This victorious multitude is presented as having overcome a great tribulation which, in the story, is yet to take place.

Occasionally, the narrator will take an inordinate amount of time describing an event which in the story does not last nearly as long. When we encounter such an occurrence, we are dealing with the question of duration of events in the story time and the discourse time. There are four different ways in which the duration of story time will be related to the duration of discourse time. These have been developed by Gérard Genette, a French narrative critic.

### 1. Summary

'... the narration in a few paragraphs or a few pages of several days, months, or years of existence, without details of action or speech' (Genette, 1980, p. 95). This means that the discourse time, which belongs to the narrator, is significantly shorter than the story time. An example of this is when a span of many years in the story is described by the writer in a sentence or two.

### 2. Pause

A pause is an instance where the story time stops while the discourse time keeps on going. It usually happens when the narrator takes time to describe something in detail. While the description takes place, the action in the story is suspended in time. When the narrator returns to the story time, no time has elapsed and we find the characters exactly where we left them.

### 3. Ellipsis

This happens when the story time keeps on going but is not presented in the discourse time. An example of this found in Revelation 20. Here, the Dragon is thrown in the pit for a thousand years, of story time. But then, a few verses later, he is out of the pit fighting against God's saints. It is then to be understood that the thousand years has passed, but nothing has been narrated of the events taking place during this thousand-year period.

### 4. Scene

A scene describes an instance where discourse time and story time are sensibly similar. The time it takes for the narrator to present the event is the same as the time needed for that event to take place. Any dialogue or utterance from a character is a good example of a scene.

## The book of Revelation: story and outline

It is important to have a general idea of what Revelation's story is in order to be able to tackle issues relating to interpretation. The following overview will enable the reader to make sense of the narrative elements which have already been addressed. Along with this overview, an outline of the book of Revelation will be provided. The reader is welcome to test this outline and add or delete any part considered relevant or not. A reader who can build an outline is usually one who has taken the time to read the story, and this is what our ultimate goal is, to have the reader tackle the text.

### An overview of Revelation's story

The story of Revelation begins with a prologue (1.1–8) introducing the author of the book, John, as well as his intended audience, the seven churches of Asia. An initial vision follows (1.9–20) in which John contemplates the figure of 'One like the Son of Man' standing among seven golden lampstands, symbols of the seven churches. This divine figure is described in a highly symbolic fashion aimed at alerting the reader to the otherworldly nature and authority of this main character. In this section, John is also ordered to write a series of letters to the seven churches previously mentioned. The main setting for this section is the island of Patmos.

John is afterward told the content of the letters which are addressed to the seven Christian congregations located in the Roman province of Asia: Ephesus, Smyrna, Pergamum, Thyatira, Sardis, Philadelphia and Laodicea (2.1 – 3.22). The seven letters share a common three-part structure. First, the one who is addressing the churches is introduced using some form of divine title, e.g., the One 'who holds the seven stars' (2.1), 'the first and the last' (2.8), the one 'who has the seven spirits of God' (3.1), etc. Next, an evaluation of each specific church is presented. The church is commended or rebuked depending on its witness to Christ's message. Finally, each letter ends with Christ promising a reward to the one who will conquer: he/she will be given permission to eat from the tree of life (2.7), will not be harmed by the second death (2.11), will be given a white stone (2.17), etc. The churches at Smyrna and Philadelphia receive unconditional praise from Christ, while the church at Laodicea is thoroughly condemned. The other four churches receive both praise and rebuke.

In the next section, the action moves to a different setting. John sees a door open in heaven (4.1) and is invited to come up and behold the events which are about to take place. John is taken, 'in the spirit' to heaven and there finds himself in God's heavenly palace. There follows an extensive description of the one who sits on the throne, as well as of the four living creatures and the twenty-four elders (4.2–11). Subsequently, John sees a scroll inscribed on the front and the back and sealed with seven seals. John despairs of finding someone who can open this scroll. He is told that 'the Lion of the tribe of Judah, the Root of David' is the one who has the power to unseal the scroll. This Lion appears as a slaughtered, yet still alive, Lamb. These last three titles (Lion, Root, Lamb) all represent Christ.

The story then continues with the opening of the seven seals (6.1 – 8.5). As the first seal is broken by the Lamb, a white horse appears. Its rider is given a crown and the power to conquer. The second seal brings out a red horse. This horse's rider is given the power to take peace away from earth. The third seal summons a black horse with a rider holding a set of scales. With the fourth seal, Death comes forth riding a pale horse. The fifth seal unveils the souls of the martyrs crying for revenge, while the sixth one provokes cosmological disasters. Before the seventh seal is open, an intercalation takes place. Intercalation is a narrative pattern also known as the 'sandwich' technique. A certain event is being narrated when suddenly a different one is introduced, developed and resolved before the story goes back to the first event. In this case, the story turns to the sealing of God's 144,000 faithful, the ones who made it through the great tribulation, before it moves back to the opening of the seventh seal (7.1–17). The seventh seal brings with it a half hour of silence, as well as heavenly worship, thunder, lightning and an earthquake.

Once the seals have been opened, the seven angels who stand in the presence of God blow seven trumpets that, once more, bring pain and suffering to earth and its citizens (8.6 – 11.19). The first trumpet brings hail and fire mixed with blood. This affects one third of the earth's soil, trees and grass. The second trumpet causes a mountain to fall into the sea and affects a third of the water and marine creatures. The third trumpet summons a falling star named Wormwood which poisons one third of the waters. The fourth trumpet spells disaster for the heavenly bodies. The last three trumpets are accompanied by woes. The fifth trumpet unleashes a fallen star (perhaps a divine being?) who unlocks the shaft of the bottomless pit and releases demonic locusts on the earth. The sixth trumpet summons four angels and their cavalry who then proceed to slaughter one third of humanity. The flow of the story is afterward interrupted by an intercalation (10.1 – 11.14). The focus moves to heaven where John is given a little scroll to eat. Afterwards, he is given a rod and asked to measure the temple of God and its altar. This is followed by God sending two witnesses who preach, are killed, resurrected and finally taken to heaven. The ascension of these two witnesses is accompanied by more calamities. The story then moves back to the seventh trumpet which, when blown, results in heavenly worship.

The next section begins with an example of flashback (12.1–18). A pregnant woman crowned with twelve stars gives birth to a male child who is taken to heaven in order to escape from a Great Red Dragon who wants to kill them both. They escape with God's help. The Dragon is afterward defeated by the angel Michael and his troops and thrown down to earth. It then summons two hideous beasts, one from the sea and one from the land, to enlist the help of earth's inhabitants in the fight against God (13.1–18). The two beasts work miracles to convince humans of their power. At that point, the story shifts to an announcement of the judgement of Babylon the Great. The One like the Son of Man reappears, this time as One ready to harvest. God's judgement is then enacted (14.1–20).

Following the previous foreshadowing of God's judgement, the story line moves once again to a septet, a series of seven events that share a similar structure and content, consisting in seven bowls which bring about seven plagues (15.1 – 16.21). The first plague causes sores, while the second and third plagues turn various bodies of water into blood. The fourth plague triggers a deadly heat wave. The fifth one affects the throne of the beast, while the sixth dries up the Euphrates. Another intercalation presents the Dragon and the beasts sending three evil spirits all over the earth to gather armies for the final battle at Armageddon (16.13–16). The seventh and final plague brings destruction to the earth once more.

The next chapters present the resolution of the main conflict. Scenes of judgement and salvation dominate this section of the book. A harlot riding a seven-headed beast is first described and clues as to her identity and that of the beast are provided (17.1–18). The fall of Babylon the Great is announced and God's faithful rejoice (18.1 – 19.10). Afterward, a white horse appears ridden by Christ who, at this time, is called 'Faithful and True' and 'The Word of God'. He does battle with the Dragon, the two beasts, and their followers. After their defeat, the beasts are thrown in the lake of fire while the Dragon is relegated to the Abyss for a thousand-year period (19.11 – 20.6).

Once the thousand-year period is over, God wins the final victory over the Dragon and its forces of evil, Gog and Magog. The Dragon is thrown into the lake of fire to be tortured forever with the two beasts.

The book of life is then opened and the final judgement takes place, including the destruction of Death and Hades (20.7–15). The denouement offers a detailed description of the New Jerusalem, the Bride of the Lamb (21.1 – 22.5). The book concludes with an epilogue assuring the reader of the worth of the prophecies it contains. This worth is based on the fact that Christ himself is the ultimate revealer of this message. The reader is finally urged to be ready for Christ's imminent coming (22.6–21).

## Outline of the book of Revelation

I. **Prologue (1.1–8)**

II. **Inaugural vision, commission to write letters, and letters (1.9 – 3.22)**
    *A.* Vision and commission to write (1.9–20)
    *B.* Letters to the seven churches of Asia (2.1 – 3.22)
        The letter to the church at Ephesus (2.1–7)
        The letter to the church at Smyrna (2.8–11)
        The letter to the church at Pergamum (2.12–17)
        The letter to the church at Thyatira (2.18–29)
        The letter to the church at Sardis (3.1–6)
        The letter to the church at Philadelphia (3.7–13)
        The letter to the church at Laodicea (3.14–22)

III. **The core of the story (4.1 – 22.5)**
    *A.* John in heaven (4.1 – 5.14)
    John's description of God, his throne, and his divine entourage (4.1–11)
    John learns about the first scroll (5.1–14)
    *B.* The seven seals (6.1 – 8.5)
    The first four seals and the horsemen (6.1–8)
    The fifth and sixth seals (6.9–17)
    **Intercalation**: The sealing of God's faithful and anticipation of final victory (7.1–17)
    The seventh seal (8.1–5)
    *C.* The seven trumpets and the three woes (8.6 – 11.19)
    The first four trumpets (8.6–13)
    The fifth trumpet and first woe (9.1–12)
    The sixth trumpet and the second woe (9.13–21)
    **Intercalation**: The little scroll, the temple measured, and the two witnesses (10.1 – 11.14)
    The seventh trumpet and third woe (11.15–19)
    *D.* A vision of Woman and Dragon (12.1–18)
    *E.* The beasts (13.1–18)

# 3

## Traditional Interpretive Approaches

### Revelation: the limits of interpretation

What could be easier than reading a story and figuring out what it means? For many people today, the question of interpretation, especially biblical interpretation, raises eyebrows and elicits comments such as: 'Why do you need to interpret Scriptures?' 'Can't you read?' Reading is often considered by the general public to be a basic skill which only requires of the reader the capacity to decode the letters, make up the words, and see their relationship to one another. This kind of mentality has spawned 'miracle' methods of reading, such as 'Hooked on Phonics'. These methods promote the practice of reading using phonetics, without any attention to the actual meaning of words, and have been driving reading specialists up the proverbial wall. Reading does seem to be an innocuous activity. However, when the act of sounding out words is brought to the next level, which is comprehension of what one is reading, the activity becomes one of the more complex acts human beings can learn to perform.

Studies have shown that the act of communicating is influenced by many intrinsic and extrinsic factors which affect the sender, the message and the receiver. When studying the sender, one has to take into consideration the background of this individual, the environment in which he/she is located, as well as the intent underlying the sending of the message. When looking at the message, one has to study its format. As for the receiver, this individual is affected by the same kind of factors as the sender. The interpretation of the message might therefore differ from what was intended by the sender. Clearly, communication and interpretation of a message might not be as easy as was once thought. This difficulty is compounded if the sender and the receiver do not belong to the same culture and time period. Therefore, interpreting any ancient document represents a daunting task.

## Where is the meaning?
### Text versus reader-based interpretations

When the act of communicating uses writing as its medium, the analysis of the end product, the text, can take many forms depending on the philosophical presuppositions which accompany the act of reading. These presuppositions relate first to the question of the nature and the role of any text. Is a text a perfect product of the intention of the writer? If answered in the affirmative, this would mean that when reading a text, one is looking at the thoughts and intentions of the author lying there on the page. If answered in the negative, it would mean that the written text is in some way different to that which the author wanted to produce, possessing a life of its own once it left the pen of the author. The debate as to the nature of any written text and the act of reading/ interpreting, which allows one to interact with such a text, can be studied using two similes often found in works dealing with theories of interpretation: Is the text a window or a mirror?

A window is made of glass which allows any one standing in front of it to see through it and observe what stands behind it. A window also reflects, in a small capacity, the image of the person standing in front of it. To compare a text to a window is to make a statement about what it can reveal to us about its author and the historical environment in which it was produced. If a text is a window, this means that we can confidently state what the author's intention was. A text is thus seen as a way of gaining information about the author's life, environment and intention. This view thus maximizes the role of the authorial intent and the *Sitz im Leben* (life situation in which the text was written) of the work, while minimizing the role of the reader.

If we apply this view to the book of Revelation, we could say that by reading the seven letters to the churches, we can gather accurate information which can help us assess the situation of the different churches of Asia in the first century. This has led many to affirm that these churches were undergoing persecution at the time when John wrote his book. However, historical data often seem to contradict the view that compares any text to a window. Consequently, if a text is not a window, allowing entry into its author's mind and his environment, what is it?

The second view, which has come to the fore in the past twenty-five years, sees the text as being a mirror. This means that when reading any text, one will likely find information which is already, consciously or unconsciously, being sought. Instead of seeing what the author wanted to present, one sees what one wants to see. The text becomes a mere reflection of the reader's own agenda. This view maximizes the role of the reader while minimizing the role of the authorial intent and the historical setting of the text. It introduces in a very forceful way the notion of bias and presuppositions in the act of reading and interpreting.

A striking example of this is found in what is known today as Historical Jesus research. A great number of scholars, from Albert Schweitzer to Dominic Crossan and N. T. Wright, have tried to recover the historical figure of the individual known as Jesus of Nazareth. In the end, these writers offered three different portraits of the same individual. Which one offered the most historically accurate depiction of Jesus? This question is still debated, since each of these writers' conclusions found proponents as well as opponents. The results of this type of research had been anticipated by George Tyrrell in his *Christianity at the Cross-Roads* (1909), in which he concluded that when peering down the well of New Testament texts, trying to find Jesus, one's own reflection would be the only thing gazing back. Is it therefore possible to gather valuable, objective, information from a text? This question leads us to address directly the problem of the locus of meaning. Does the meaning of a text reside in the author's intent, the textual end product, the reader, or somewhere in between?

## Author, text, and reader as sources of meaning

The past thirty years have witnessed an increasing debate as to the source of meaning in written communication. Three basic approaches have been proposed. The first one locates the meaning of a written work in the intention of the author, faithfully transmitted through the text. The second school of thought affirms that the meaning resides with the reader alone. A third approach presents the possibility of involving both the author/text and the reader.

The traditional way of interpreting a text was to try and find as much information as possible about the author who produced the work. The meaning of the text was considered to be directly linked to the history of the writer at the time of its creation. In order to have the tools needed to interpret the text, one had to identify where the writer was and what his/her emotional, psychological, economic and relational status were at the time. Any erroneous interpretation was blamed on a lack of historical knowledge. In the case of the book of Revelation, one had to find as much information as possible about the writer John. The history of interpretive practice, however, has tended to prove that this search for the author's intention was lacking, since it is almost impossible to perfectly identify the intention of any individual, past or contemporary.

A derivative approach later surfaced. This theory stipulated that the text held an interpretive potential waiting to be actualized. The reader would therefore come to the text and extract the meaning lying within it. The text would thus control its own interpretation. The more 'in tune' one got with the text, the greater the capacity to offer an interpretation which would not violate the meaning residing in it. An erroneous interpretation was considered to be the result of the lack of relevant experience on the part of the reader.

The presence of varied and sometimes contradictory interpretations of the same written work gave rise to another approach to reading and interpreting. This time, the reader was confirmed as sole source of meaning. Each reader would come to the text and take from it what he/she was inputting. Without the presence of the reader, the text meant nothing; it did not hold any meaning on its own. Meaning became purely and solely a function of the reader. Every interpretation could thus be considered as valid. What one read in the text was validated only by one's own experiences, presuppositions and needs. In the case of Revelation, this meant that any interpretation of its symbols could be considered right. Some could thus say that 666 represented Nero Caesar, while others would say that it was the Pope, and still others only a symbol with no specific referent. According to the reader-centred theory of interpretation, all of these would be correct. This approach faced a wave of criticism accusing it of emptying the text of its substance and violating the original intention of the author. If a text could mean anything, it might as well mean nothing.

A new approach then came along, as an alternative to the ones already presented. It emphasized the role of the reader *and* the text in the interpretive task. An interpretation would be considered valid if it met certain constraints or limits present in the text. This can be illustrated by looking at one of the seven letters to the churches of Asia. John addressed these communities in the first century. Any interpretation that would take the church of Philadelphia in Revelation as representing the Christian community living in the city of Philadelphia, Pennsylvania, USA in 2000 would be considered invalid since it would violate a historical and geographical constraint present in the text itself. This third approach thus stands midway between the text-centred and reader-centred theories of reading.

What to think of all this? Which approach will allow one to read and interpret Revelation as it was meant to be? The answer is not an easy one. One should, I believe, aim for balance and respect of all the parties involved, the author, the text and the reader. Texts, especially ancient texts, are open to various interpretations. It is the role of the community to which each reader belongs (community of readers) to offer guidelines and tools to equip each and every one of its members with the skills and knowledge required to bring about the best interpretation of any text. All through our textual encounters, we must remain aware of the boundaries and possibilities present in every act of reading. Since no text allows only one reading, and not every reading is always valid, reader beware: 'Texts control readings, but so do readers' (Barr, 1998, p. 23).

## Yesterday, today or tomorrow? History-based interpretations

### Who's Got The Truth? A history of conflicting interpretations

A brief historical overview of Revelation's interpretation often leaves one dazed and confused. Who was right? Who actually found the key to the prophecies and symbols of the Apocalypse? Since the second century of our era, opposite interpretations have laid claim to the truth residing in this work of biblical literature. The first main conflict in interpretation took place in the second and third centuries.

The heart of the conflict concerning the correct interpretation of Revelation was part of a larger antagonism between two Christian communities of interpreters: Antioch, in Syria; and Alexandria, in Egypt. Each group had its star theologians defending the community's interpretive method and criticizing their opponents'. The community of Antioch was known for its literal interpretation of Scriptures. The text was its own interpreter. One simply had to read what was written down on the parchment and accept that this was it. According to this school of thought, there was nothing more to be done.

At the other end of the interpretive spectrum stood the Alexandrian school of thought, represented by its star pupil, Origen. This Christian community was very uneasy with a literal interpretation of Scriptures, especially with a literal reading of Revelation. Not only did they find some images completely absurd, like a rider with a sword coming out of his mouth, but they considered some to be dangerous. They were especially worried with a literal interpretation of the millennium found in Revelation 20. This had already led some literalist interpreters to describe the millennium in very sensual terms, stressing the satisfaction of the various appetites. In order to counter this tendency, the school of Alexandria proposed an allegorical interpretation of Scriptures. Each passage was considered as having various spiritual meanings which were the ones to be sought by the believers. An example of this was Origen's interpretation of the seven heads of the beast (Rev 13.1), as representing the seven deadly sins. Everything had to be interpreted allegorically. This, according to the Alexandrians, was the way of finding the truth in Revelation.

This debate between a literal interpretation of the images and prophecies found in Revelation, and a symbolic, allegorical one has been perpetuated throughout Christian history, down to this day and age. As history unfolded, this debate spawned four ways of interpreting Revelation. The easiest way of assessing these methods is by looking at how each relates Revelation's images and prophecies to the historical flow. These four approaches are: the preterist, the historicist, the futurist and the idealist. For each of these methods we will examine the following elements: presuppositions, basic interpretive framework and underlying historical factors.

## The preterist

The first interpretive approach to be examined is mostly favoured by mainline Christian denominations, Roman Catholic, Anglican, Presbyterian, etc. However, historically speaking, it was not the first approach devised to interpret Revelation. On the contrary, it was one of the latest. The word 'preterist' is derived from 'preterit' meaning past tense. This method is also called contemporary-historical, historical or historical-critical. The basic relation of this method to the historical flow is easily identifiable.

The preterist interpretation focuses mainly on the historical context in which Revelation was written. It considers the author John and his audience to be central to any interpretive effort. Looking at the various prophecies contained in the book of Revelation, the preterist argues that these were all fulfilled at some point in the past. Two variants of the preterist method can be identified. The first one sees most of Revelation's prophecies as having been fulfilled at the time of the destruction of the temple of Jerusalem in 70. To support this argument, the preterist interpreters point to several passages considered to be referring directly to the rule of the emperor Nero Caesar as contemporary to the writing of the book (6.2; 13.1–18; 17.1–3). The letters to the churches are considered to be describing local conditions which fit the pre-70 Christian context best. Additionally, chapter 11 seems to present the temple in Jerusalem as still standing at the time of writing. The second version of the preterist approach understands most events in Revelation to have taken place at the fall both of Jerusalem in the first century, and of Rome in the fifth century.

The preterist approach, therefore, considers that the book of Revelation was written in order to comfort Christians who were suffering both from imperial pressure to engage in emperor worship and persecution from official Judaism which considered them a nuisance and a dangerous sect. Consequently, the prophecies of Revelation are interpreted as pointing to God's judgement on official Judaism, enacted through the destruction of its centre of worship; and the Roman empire, through its demise at the hands of barbarians. This approach is thus very critical of any interpretation that does not take seriously the historical situation responsible for the book being written. In order fully to interpret the prophecies and events presented in Revelation, one must gather as much historical information on the writer John, the seven churches of Asia, and the political-religious situation that prevailed in Palestine, and the Roman empire in general, during the first century.

Preterism, as an interpretive method, was born of the conflict between the churches of the Reformation and the Roman Catholic Church. One of the mainstays of Reformation interpretation of Revelation was the identification of the papacy, or a specific pope, as the Antichrist described in John's work. Facing the growing and constant threat of the Reformation movement, which had been spreading like wildfire, the Roman Catholic Church took it upon itself to interpret Revelation in a way which would deny or contradict the claims laid upon it by the Reformers. This counter-attack was done through the use of an extremely historical approach to the hermeneutical task. In this way, the Roman Church prefigured modern interpretations of the book of Revelation. The Jesuit interpreters, Ribeira (1537–91) and Alcasar (1554–1613), were hard at work proving that Revelation was not written to predict the future, and that the pope was not the Antichrist. For like-minded interpreters, Revelation's worth was in the information it could provide about the Christian communities for which it was originally written. Revelation was therefore considered as having been written by John for the benefit of specific first-century Christian communities, very much like Paul's letters. This is still today the backbone of the preterist approach.

The main strength of the preterist approach is that it takes seriously the historical background of the book of Revelation. It emphasizes the fact that the book had to make sense to the communities receiving it: 'The interpreter assumes that legitimate interpretation must be responsible to and derived from the meaning the text had for its original readers, even if it does not simply repeat it' (Boring, 1989, p. 51). The major weakness of the preterist interpretation stems from its inability to deal adequately with the description of the final, ultimate, victory of Christ as depicted in Revelation. If the prophecies were all fulfilled in the end of the first or the fifth century, how come Christians had to face so many persecutions in the centuries that followed? Preterist interpreters often have to step out of their own interpretive framework in order to answer such questioning.

## The historicist

The second traditional approach to Revelation is known as the historicist, also called church-historical, continuous-historical, or world-historical. This view was extremely popular in the early church and reached its apex during the period of the Reformation in the sixteenth century. Today, it is used mainly by conservative, mostly fundamentalist, churches. This view tends to resurface and gain popularity in times of international crisis, as during the Gulf war of 1991. Doomsayers and would-be messiahs, like David Koresh, favoured this approach above all others.

The basic premise of this interpretive method is that the prophecies found in chapters 4–22 of the book of Revelation are considered to be symbolic predictions of the unfolding of history all the way to the time of the interpreter. One has to decipher what the symbols mean by relating them to historical events and characters. The underlying assumption of this approach is that the interpreter is living in the time just before the return of Christ and the consummation of history. One of the very first commentators on Revelation, Victorinus of Pettau (c. 300), was a proponent of this method. He considered himself as living in the period of time represented by the sixth seal. The seventh seal would usher in the end of time. However, the greatest representative of this approach was a Cistercian monk by the name of Joachim of Fiore (c. 1135–1202). He wrote the first complete historicist interpretation of the Apocalypse. Joachim maintained that the symbols found in the book of Revelation were linked to historical events which had already taken place and gave veiled information as to what would happen in the future. His work would be mirrored by countless groups and individuals in the next eight centuries.

The basic flaw of this approach is that it is very much centred around the world of the interpreter. The book loses its historical value for the communities of the first century for which it was written. Only the seven letters of chapters 2–3 are considered by the historicist interpreter to have been addressed to communities of the first century. It is therefore puzzling to think of what use the book would have been for Christians living in all the centuries preceding the time of the interpreter. What would have been the didactic or moral value, for a first-century Christian, to know that one day a beast with seven heads, known as the Warsaw Pact or the European Community, would turn against the followers of the Christ. Or, even more, that the mark of the beast would materialize as computerized bank cards, or the universal product code.

As the aforementioned examples have shown, this interpretive method has generated endless interpretations, one more fanciful than the other. The problem remains that interpreters using this approach seldom agree with one another, basically invalidating the method. In a fast-changing world situation like ours, contemporary doomsayers who favour this approach are always involved in a constant revision of their predictions. This is great for selling countless editions of one's work, but it does not hold water in the face of serious questioning. Another flaw in this method is that, according to most historicist interpreters, Revelation described events which took place only in Western, mostly European, history. Parochialism is rampant. The main strength of this approach is that it takes the prophetic, understood as predictive, aspect of Revelation seriously. However, the many weaknesses of the historicist method have led to a steady decline in its use since the time of the Enlightenment.

## The futurist

The futurist approach is also known as end-historical, dispensationalist, eschatological, and premillennialist. This interpretive method as been a mainstay of conservative evangelical Christian churches. The academic headquarters from which it is disseminated today is Dallas Theological Seminary in the United States of America. The major tenet of this interpretive framework is that the prophecies found in chapters 4 – 22 of Revelation belong to a not so distant future. The seven churches named in chapters 2 – 3 are not only historical churches of the first century, but represent seven distinct periods of church history often called dispensations. The events in chapters 4 – 22 belong to the seventh dispensation and are awaiting the end times to be fulfilled. These prophecies are considered as describing in detail two periods, one which will last for seven years before the return of Christ, and a second one which will last one thousand years after Christ's return, the millennium of Revelation 20.

Many interpreters who hold to this approach see themselves as living in the sixth dispensation, the penultimate step to the consummation of history. The contemporary church is to be identified with the Laodicean church, the church which Christ is about to spit out (Rev 3.16). This approach was used in its basic form by early church fathers such as Irenaeus and Justin Martyr. It was however given its full shape by a group of Christian believers known as dispensationalists.

Dispensationalists held to a literal interpretation of prophetic Scripture. This approach is also very much linked to another theological system known as premillennialism. The first premillennialists believed that the world was on a straight road to final destruction and that God would put an end to it before the thousand-year reign of Christ. The first main proponent of premillennialism, and of dispensationalism according to some, was John Nelson Darby (1800–82). His views were exported to America and popularized by Cyrus Scofield (1843–1921), who taught at what was to become Dallas Theological Seminary. He published the *Scofield Reference Bible*, a Bible with footnotes emphasizing the dispensationalist interpretation. According to Scofield, a dispen-sation is 'a period of time during which man is tested in respect of obedience to some specific revelation of the will of God' (Scofield, 1909, note to Gen 1.28). Most central also to the futurist approach is the question of the tribulation in Revelation 7. Premillennialists believe that Christ will keep his saints from experiencing this tribulation by taking them up to heaven to be with him. This is known as the rapture.

This approach exists today in two versions: classical dispensationalism and progressive dispensationalism. Classical dispensationalism bases its reading on a literal interpretation of the prophecies found in chapters 4 – 22. Verse 1.19, 'Now write what you have seen, what is, and what is to take place after this' becomes representative of the structure of the book. 'What you have seen' is taken as referring back to John's vision of Christ in chapter 1. 'What is' points to the seven letters of chapters 2 – 3; and 'what is to take place after this' to chapters 4 – 22. Classical dispensationalists also believe that the absence of the word 'church' from chapter 4 onwards means that it has already been taken to heaven to be with Christ and to await the end of it all. This form of the futurist interpretation is basically pessimistic. Even if world affairs are going well, a great catastrophe is awaited which will plunge the world into the last dispensation. The final events will then unfold in the same order as the visions found in chapters 4 – 22: restoration of the nation of Israel to its land, the rapture, a tribulation lasting seven years, the Antichrist's reign, Armageddon, the Second Coming, Christ's thousand-year reign, the final battle against Satan, and Christ's victory and eternal reign with his saints.

The second version of the futurist approach is known as modified futurism or progressive dispensationalism. It emphasizes the 'already/ not yet' aspect of the kingdom of God. Christ's reign began at the resurrection and some of the visions have already started being realized. This version is more optimistic than the classical one. However, it does agree with its predecessor on all the major points: restoration of ethnic Israel, premillennialism, the rapture, and the Great Tribulation.

As for the preceding methods that we have examined, this approach exhibits some strengths and some weaknesses. Its strength resides in its eschatological focus and its certainty that history does hold a divine purpose which will be fulfilled in time. As Robert Mounce said: 'With the futurist we must agree that the central message of the book is eschatological, and to whatever extent the End has been anticipated in the course of history, it yet remains as the one great climactic point toward which all history moves' (1998, p. 29). This approach also takes seriously the prophetic aspect of the book of Revelation. Finally, its eschatological thrust is very comforting to believers since it emphasizes the final victory of good over evil.

The main weakness of this approach is that it makes most of Revelation irrelevant to its first audience. It also downplays the epistolary and apocalyptic nature of the book. Its interpretation of the nature of prophecy has also been criticized. The most negative aspect of this method has been illustrated repeatedly by televangelists and the gurus of pop-eschatology *à la* Jack Van Impe. The well-known American televangelist Jerry Falwell, on 2 February 1999, predicted the coming of the Antichrist in the next ten years, triggering the rapture. An earlier example of this longing for the end was found in Hal Lindsey's 1970s bestseller *The Late Great Planet Earth*. The pessimism of the approach and its alarmist tendency do not convey the basic optimism that stands at the heart of the Christian faith. The notion of rapture, a small group being whisked away to safety while the rest suffer, also evokes an almost sectarian mindset that is barely Christian. Every world crisis is interpreted as the beginning of the end; which inevitably fails to materialize. The approach might also be seen as advocating some form of catastrophic event such as a global nuclear war. Christians who hold to this interpretation might feel justified to remain passive in the face of a severe crisis, instead of contributing to its solution. The rise of progressive dispensationalism might help remove some of these weaknesses; but only time will tell.

## The idealist

The last of the traditional approaches to Revelation is known as the idealist, symbolic, non-historical or spiritual. This is one of the oldest ways of interpreting Revelation. It is directly linked to the exegetical method which was practiced in the Christian community of Alexandria, Egypt. This method was known as allegorical interpretation. As stated previously in this chapter, the basic premise of the allegorical method was that the literal meaning of Scriptures represented only a very small part of its real significance. One had to probe deeper and uncover the spiritual truths concealed behind the words. This led to a sometime fanciful interpretation of Scriptures, especially Revelation. The allegorical interpretation played a major role in getting Revelation to be kept as part of the Christian canon. Many believers were extremely 'turned off' by the sometimes violent and gory images of the Apocalypse. The allegorical interpretation allowed these same images to be transformed into something more palatable, more acceptable.

This approach became the dominant interpretive framework used to read Revelation all the way to the time of the Reformation. After having been eclipsed by the historicist method favoured by the Reformers, it made a comeback with the Enlightenment. The idealist approach became linked to a form of millenarian belief known as postmillennialism. Postmillennialists believed that social progress would not be stopped and that only at the end of such a positive progression of history would Christ come back. The images and events of Revelation were therefore emptied of any possible historical content and interpreted symbolically. Eighteenth-century proponents of post-millennialism included Daniel Whitby (1638–1726), Jonathan Edwards (1703–58), and Samuel Hopkins (1721–1803).

The idealist interpretation has perpetuated the allegorical tradition of Clement and Origen of Alexandria, and the intrinsic optimism of postmillennialism. This approach interprets the book of Revelation in a symbolic, spiritual way. None of the images and events found in the book are linked to any specific historical event, past, present or future. The proponents of this method find in Revelation a source of universal, timeless truths which relate to the Christian experience in general, i.e., God wants us to be faithful, good always prevails in the end, etc. The overall idealist interpretation of Revelation is that of a symbolic representation of the fight between good and evil taking place in every human being.

The strength of this approach is that it makes Revelation relevant for today's reader. The book is not seen as being chained down to any specific historical referent. Therefore, the meaning can be universalized and individualized. Existentialist interpretations of the symbols often abound within this approach. However, like all the other approaches previously studied, it does contain serious flaws. The first such weakness is similar to that found in the futurist and the historicist interpretations. It has to do with making the book irrelevant for its first-century readers. If Revelation does not contain any historical referential content, its value for the first Christian communities to whom it was addressed is severely compromised. This approach also denies the epistolary and prophetic character of Revelation. By transforming Revelation into something more palatable to some

Christians, the idealist interpretation robs the whole book of its edge. Revelation becomes a shapeless amalgam of universal truths applied to the believers' life in such an individualistic way as to become completely foreign to the biblical idea of faith and community.

## Would the real interpretation of Revelation please stand up?

After reading about the four historical approaches to Revelation, and reflecting critically on each of them, one might be left wondering as to which method actually carries the greatest interpretive potential. This is still hotly debated today. The only approach that seems on the brink of completely disappearing is the historicist. The other three are still thriving among the Christian masses and the scholarly world. Evangelical churches still hold firmly to the futurist interpretation in its classical dispensationalist guise, with the progressive dispensationalist slowly making headway. The Roman Catholic Church, as well as most other 'mainline' denominations, hold to a basically preterist approach which incorporates elements of the idealist method. The mixed way of interpreting Revelation is rapidly gaining ground, especially in the scholarly world. Many interpreters are realizing that Revelation describes historical events while at the same time underlying things that will always hold true for the Christian believer. Add to this the eschatological thrust of the futurist approach, and you might just get the kind of hybrid, multi-pronged, method which could allow Revelation finally to unveil all of its meaning. Only time will tell which approach is right, if any.

# 4

## Key Images and Themes: An Exercise in Interpretation

The preceding chapter, on the methods traditionally used to interpret Revelation, has highlighted the variety of opinions present in the Christian community concerning this specific part of Scripture. The present chapter endeavours to provide an overview of some significant images and themes that have become a mainstay of studies on the Apocalypse of John, namely: the question of the genre of Revelation – apocalyptic, prophetic, or epistolary; authorship and dating, structure and interpretation of symbols. The intent is to offer a fair description of the various opinions on these topics. This will hopefully allow the reader to gain insight into the value of the various interpretations proposed by the myriad of works, past and present, written on the last book of the Bible.

### 'Revelation of Jesus Christ': Revelation and apocalyptic literature

#### Revelation and the question of genre

What is the difference between reading a report from the Stock Exchange, William Wordsworth's poem *Ode: Intimations of Immortality*, and Stephen King's novel *The Shining*? Some would say that it is obvious. A report from the Dow Jones in New York would be consulted with the intent of seeing which stocks are trading well, what the volume of trading is, and where the economy is going. Wordsworth's poetic work would be read mostly as an example of beautiful, romantic poetry; and Stephen King's novel as a chilling, disturbing masterpiece of horror. Three words are to be highlighted here: report, poem, novel. These terms belong to a concept of literary criticism known as genre. Genre is the answer to the question: 'Why doesn't any reader approach these three documents in the same way, with the same frame of mind, and the same expectations?' One would surely be looked at in a very inquisitive way if found reciting the Dow Jones' trade numbers on the corner of Wall street with the feverish emotional fervour and intonation of a thespian declaiming one of Shakespeare's soliloquies. The same reaction would meet anyone trying to pass King's *The Shining* as a scientific study of the effects of isolation on the left side of the brain. What is a genre? How do we identify it? And what does this have to do with the book of Revelation?

Simply defined, a genre is a form, type, or kind of writing. We know, almost instinctively of genres such as novel, folk tale, poem, etc. If we were to delve a little deeper into the nature of the concept of genre, we could say that it represents 'a group of written texts marked by distinctive recurring characteristics which constitute a recognizable and coherent type of writing' (Collins, 1979, p. 1). This definition basically states that a number of written works possess many common traits. This set of shared elements allows a reader to classify a certain text into a specific family, which is called the genre.

The main advantage in being able to categorize any piece of writing is that it allows the reader to come to any work with the correct interpretive lens or set of expectations: 'An awareness of the form or genre of a work programs our encounter with it' (Ryken, 1992, p. 208). Through the category of genre, we learn what to expect of a text and get help in our effort to interpret it correctly. In the case of the book of Revelation, the issue of its genre has been strongly debated. Three main contenders have been identified: apocalypse, prophecy and letter.

## Defining the apocalyptic genre

The first genre within which the book of Revelation is often filed is that of apocalyptic literature or apocalypse. The word 'apocalypse' as designating a genre, comes from Revelation 1.1 *Apocalypsis Iesou Christou*, 'The revelation of Jesus Christ ...' The word 'revelation' is one possible translation of the Greek word *apocalypsis* which can also be translated as 'apocalypse'. The basic meaning is that of unveiling or revealing. Many definitions of this genre have been offered through the years. One of these was developed by the members of the Society of Biblical Literature, an international group of biblical scholars. A short analysis of it should help clarify some of its more technical features.

Apocalypse can be defined as:

> a genre of revelatory literature with a narrative framework, in which a revelation is mediated by an otherworldly being to a human recipient, disclosing a transcendent reality which is both temporal, insofar as it

envisages eschatological salvation, and spatial insofar as it involves another, supernatural world. (Collins, 1979, p. 9).

[It was] intended to interpret present, earthly circumstances in light of the supernatural world and of the future, and to influence both the understanding and the behavior of the audience by means of divine authority. (Yarbro Collins, 1986, p. 7)

An apocalypse is first of all *revelatory literature*, meaning a form of writing which includes a *revelation*, a giving out of knowledge which was hidden but is now to be uncovered. This writing possesses a *narrative framework*, a story-like structure. This knowledge is offered to a human seer, a visionary, through the help of an intermediary, an in-between agent, who very often is an angel or some other supernatural being. The content of this revelation describes a *transcendent reality*, things which are out of this world. This reality is both *temporal* and *spatial*. It is *temporal* because it deals with the end of time, with the salvation which will take place at the end of history, and *spatial* since it talks about a different place, a supernatural world.

The second part of the definition presents what an apocalypse was meant to accomplish. It was supposed to give meaning to events happening in the present by looking at them from the point of view of God (or the gods) and the end of history. This, in turn, was supposed to help the recipients of this revelation understand these same events and alter their way of behaving. This message received its authority from its divine origin.

## Revelation and Jewish apocalyptic literature

The term 'apocalypse' taken from Revelation 1.1, has become the generic title given to a series of works which resemble the book of Revelation in form and content. The writer John, however, did not invent this style of writing. It can be found in many cultures, including Persian, Hellenistic and Jewish. In fact, the greatest number of apocalypses that have been identified to this day belong to Judaism. When looking at the Hebrew Scriptures in the Bible, we can identify several portions of books as being apocalypses. The most typical is found in the book of Daniel, chapters 7 – 12. Other passages are found in the books of the prophets Isaiah (24 – 27; 56 – 66), Ezekiel (38 – 39), Joel (3 – 4), and Zechariah (9 – 14). The majority of apocalyptic works, however, are not to be found in the Bible but in a group of writings called pseudepigrapha; a series of documents put under the name of someone other than their actual writer.

Apocalyptic literature is considered as having arisen out of the phenomenon of prophecy. The Jewish apocalypses we possess were written between 200 BCE and 100 CE. The main changes in Israel's political and religious situation after the return from the Babylonian exile, around 538 BCE, brought along a new set of questions which led to the use of apocalyptic writing. Some of these questions had to do with the fact that the promises made by the prophets had not taken place. There was no Messiah, there was no new David, no political independence, etc. Even more, around 165 BCE the Israelites had to endure persecution from their Hellenistic masters. People were being brutally killed because of their faith. Where was God during such times? What had happened to the covenant between the Lord and his people? Prophecy having slowly faded out of Israel's religious landscape, apocalyptic thinking and writing moved in to fill the void. The break between prophecy and apocalyptic was not as clean as one might like to think. Apocalyptic appeared as an adaptation and development of prophecy for new times and new challenges to the faith.

Apocalypses, as a specific literary genre, exhibit many typical features. In order to consider the book of Revelation as an apocalypse, one should be able to identify within it some of these elements. The following is a short, selective, list of components which are considered to be common to the genre of apocalypse. References from the book of Revelation will be highlighted so as to confirm the presence of any given element.

### a) Visions
A series of visions compose the one main vision report found between Rev 4.1 – 22.9. The expression 'I saw' surfaces repeatedly 1.12–13; 5.1; 6.1, etc. These visions are often accompanied by auditions identified by the expression 'I heard' (5.11, 13; 6.1–7; 7.4; 8.13, etc.). John's visionary experience was thus a 'multimedia' one.

### b) Otherworldly journey
The seer is presented as being taken to heaven and allowed to gaze at the heavenly courts. In many Jewish apocalypses, the seer goes through several levels of heaven until he gets to a point where he is not allowed to go any further. In Revelation, John is allowed to gaze at the throne of God (4.1ff.) and his vision oscillates between heaven and earth.

### c) Presence of a heavenly mediator and interpreter
Many Jewish apocalypses have an angel playing the role of interpreter of visions to the human seer. In Revelation, this angelic mediator is present (1.2; 22.8–16) but does not play as extensive a role in interpreting the visions as that observed in Jewish apocalyptic.

## d) Pseudonymity

All Jewish apocalypses were pseudonymous. This means that each book was given the name of an ancient Bible character like Enoch, Ezra, Baruch, Isaiah, Abraham, etc. Such a procedure seems to have been a way to insure authority for these documents at a time when prophets were not around any more and the Law of Moses had become the only accepted point of reference in regard to God's revelation. This element is absent from the book of Revelation. The writer John did mention his name.

## e) Prophecy after the fact

One of the elements found in Jewish apocalypses is that of events being prophesied after they have actually occurred. According to a large number of scholars, the book of Daniel is a good example of this. In the opinion of these same scholars, the book was written at the time of the revolt of the Maccabees around 165 BCE. By putting the setting of the story back in the time of the Babylonian exile, the writer was able to present all the events that took place between 587 BCE and his own time, around 165 BCE as prophecies made by the fictional character of Daniel. This is like betting on a horse after the race has already taken place and going to the cashier to get the winning money. Since all the 'after the fact' prophecies are presented as having been fulfilled, the reader's confidence in regard to predictions made by the writer concerning the real future would be bolstered. This element is mostly absent from the book of Revelation.

## f) Use of metaphors and symbols

The book of Revelation is replete with strange animals (four living beings, beast with seven heads and ten horns), mythological creatures (Dragon), and powerful images (Harlot drunk with the blood of the saints, rider with a sword coming out of his mouth). In this, it is thoroughly apocalyptic.

## g) Extensive use of numbers and colours

Numbers and colours play a major role in the book of Revelation. We encounter red, white, black and yellowish-green horses; a red dragon, saints dressed in white. A Harlot is dressed in scarlet. Numbers abound: 3, 4, 7, 1000, 144,000, 666.

## h) Dualism

Apocalypses have a strong tendency to be dualistic, to divide everything in two categories: good or bad, divine or human, heavenly or earthly. There are no shades of grey. Revelation shares this outlook. The evil forces of the earthly world are out to get the faithful of the Lord who, in heaven, are already presented as being victorious.

The above mentioned elements represent only a small number of components which are considered to form the literary genre of apocalypse. Due to the absence of pseudonymity, after-the-fact prophecy, and lack of interpretation of most visions, the apocalyptic character of Revelation is sometimes downplayed. It is true that John's work is Christian in nature and stemmed from a different outlook than its Jewish counterpart. John did not need to use pseudonymity, since the authority of his revelation came from God Himself. He did not need to use after-the-fact prophecies to assure his readers of God's victory since this same victory had already taken place in the death and resurrection of Jesus. The majority opinion, however, sees Revelation as an apocalypse. Nonetheless, the prophetic character of Revelation is not to be denied.

## 'The words of the prophecy': Revelation and prophecy

The second genre which is often used to interpret the book of Revelation is that of prophecy. Interpreters who tend to minimize the importance of Revelation as apocalypse often highlight what they consider to be the essentially prophetic nature of this book. This identification is mainly based on information found in the text itself. Revelation 1.3 states 'Blessed is the one who reads aloud the words of the prophecy ...' In 19.10, the angel tells John that 'the testimony of Jesus is the spirit of prophecy'. In chapter 22, the book is presented four times in the context of prophecy, either as 'the words of the prophecy of this book' (vv. 7–10) or as 'the words of the book of this prophecy' (vv. 18–19). These strongly suggest that the prophetic label has been intended by the author himself. The prophetic vocation of John appears to be implied by his first vision of Christ when he is ordered to 'Write in a book what you see and send it to the seven churches' (1.11). In 10.11 he is ordered to 'prophesy again'. Finally, in 22.9, the angel tells John: 'I am a fellow servant with you and your comrades the prophets.' John is, by association, identified as a prophet. There are therefore a number of internal elements pointing to Revelation as representing the end product of John's prophetic activity.

If prophecy is accepted as a way of analysing Revelation, some concepts will need further definition. What kind of prophet was John? One like the great prophets of Israel's history? Or was he a Christian prophet? If so, was he a community prophet or an itinerant one? These questions need to be answered in order to get a better understanding of the issues involved in identifying the book of Revelation as prophecy.

## Revelation and Old Testament prophecy

The prophetic books occupy a large place in the Hebrew Scriptures. They include the twelve minor prophets, such as Amos, Hosea, Habakkuk, Malachi, etc.; as well as the towering figures of Isaiah, Jeremiah and Ezekiel. Other prophets, like Elijah and Elisha, do not have books in their names but still play a considerable role in the Bible stories. Prophecy was an integral part of Israelite religious life. The prophet was an individual who through a personal spiritual experience felt called by God to proclaim God's message. The prophet of God did not decide to become a prophet, he was chosen.

When comparing the prophetic books of the Hebrew Scriptures, various common elements can be identified. The presence of these same elements in the book of Revelation has sometimes resulted in its genre being identified as prophetic instead of apocalyptic. The following are some of the components of classical prophecy that can be identified as being present in the book of Revelation:

### *Call and commission*
The prophet beholds the glory of God in a vision and receives a personal message, through vision and audition, that he must now go and proclaim. Isaiah 6.1–9 and Jeremiah 1.4–10 exemplify the typical call and commission narrative.

The book of Revelation contains something similar. In 1.9–20, John receives the command to write and send the message to seven churches. As well, he contemplates the glory of Christ resurrected and falls like dead only to be strengthened by the hand of Christ himself and is told again to write down what is about to happen. This first call and commission narrative is compounded by the one found later in chapter 10 where John is confronted by a powerful angel, described in a Christ-like manner, and given a little scroll to eat as in Ezekiel 3.1–3.

### *Messenger formula*
The messenger formula was a way for the prophet to indicate that his message was in reality the words of God. The expression 'Thus says the Lord' with its variants, was used by the prophets to emphasize this notion. In the book of Revelation, the expressions 'these are the words of …' (2.8, 18; 3.7)and 'these are the words of him' (2.1, 12; 3.1), as well as, 'these things says the Amen, the faithful and true witness …' (3.14) seem to mimic the prophetic messenger formula. This was used to emphasize that, through John's writing, Christ himself was speaking to the churches.

The presence of the above elements, as well as many others, does build a strong argument that Revelation includes classical prophecy in its genre. The question is to what extent. Is it all prophecy or is this just an add-on to the main apocalyptic genre? Furthermore, what is the link between John's type of prophecy and that found in the Hebrew Scriptures? The answer to this last question forces one to examine the historical phenomenon of Christian prophecy.

## Revelation and Christian prophecy

Christian prophecy is still a relatively difficult concept to study due to the small number of ancient documents that mention it. We do know from Paul's letters, and a few other Christian documents, that prophets exercised their ministry in the first Christian communities. These prophets were either itinerant or belonged to a specific community. They communicated the message of the risen Christ to the believers. Their outlook was different from that of the classical Hebrew prophets due to the already present victory of God gained through the death and resurrection of Jesus. They did not have to announce the coming of a Messiah, the Lord's anointed. It had already happened. The Day of the Lord had already dawned through the cross and the empty tomb.

As a Christian prophet, John's goal was not to interpret the Hebrew Scriptures but to present the message of the risen Christ to the seven communities of Asia. This might explain why John, in his use of Old Testament texts, never once quoted directly any of the passages he used. His whole prophetic ministry was founded upon the authority and revelation of the Lord Jesus Christ and centred around his imminent return. The outlook was therefore completely Christian. It is interesting to note that the book of Revelation itself presents Christian prophets in action, especially in opposition to John's message. In 2.20, a prophetess, pejoratively named Jezebel, is introduced along with her followers. Another group, the Nicolaitans, (2.6, 15) seems to have also been engaged in prophetic activity. But was this prophecy a blueprint of the future?

## Revelation and predictive prophecy

Our last point, concerning prophecy in Revelation, has to do with the nature and role of prophetic activity. Two opinions are generally held. The first one defines prophecy as the presentation of God's word within the present situation, with an eye out for the immediate future. This is what most Old Testament scholars consider prophecy to have been. The prophet was not asked to predict the future, but to address the religious, social, and political problems of the community. The original meaning of the word 'prophet' included the idea of speaking on behalf of someone else. When examining the role played by the Israelite prophets, we realize that God sent them with an urgent message which usually had to do with conversion, letting go of pagan idolatry, and coming back to the one, true God. If the individuals addressed did not repent and turn back to God, consequences would ensue. However, these consequences laid in the near, not the distant, future.

When Jeremiah prophesied, in the name of God, the fall of Jerusalem at the hand of the Babylonians, his message was not a prediction à la Nostradamus. It was a realistic analysis of the dire consequences which would follow a refusal simply to surrender to the Babylonians and let God do the rest. Nonetheless, most prophets did look to the future, to a time when Israel would live in peace and prosperity under the aegis of a new David, the Lord's anointed, the promised Messiah. However, this seems to have been the sole extent of their outlook on the future.

Many of the prophecies which Christians considered to have been predictive of the long-term future, as in the Immanuel prophecy of Isaiah 7.14, were in fact rereadings of these passages through the lens of the Jesus event. Therefore, the prophecies of John's Revelation should be considered as messages the seer was delivering to the seven communities of Asia to help them deal with their present condition. Any application of these same messages to a distant future would be an after-effect of the nature of the symbolic language used to describe the visions. Such an interpretation of the nature and role of prophecy considers as invalid the use of John's prophecies in order to predict what the future of humanity and the Church will look like. A prophecy is not a blueprint of the future but a divine message dealing with the here and now of its original audience. This view of prophecy is held mostly by interpreters who favour the preterist and/or idealist approaches to Revelation (Roloff, Aune, Krodel, Schüssler Fiorenza, Ford, Rowland, Beale, Boring, Yarbro Collins).

The second view of the nature and role of prophecy in the book of Revelation holds strongly to the predictive element of such activity. Proponents of this view emphasize that the meaning of the word prophet is not only 'speaking for', as mouthpiece of God; but 'forth-teller', as in predicting the future (Thomas, 1992, pp. 25–9). When reading a passage like Isaiah 7.14, they consider the prophet as having actually predicted the virginal conception experienced by Mary and Jesus' subsequent birth.

The book of Revelation is thus seen by supporters of this approach as a prediction of what will take place in the future of the Church. The main question addressed to those who hold this position is that of the relevance of the book for the original hearers/readers. Why would a first-century Christian bother reading a work which presented what would take place in two thousand years or more? How would that help a community facing oppression because of its Christian faith? This analysis of predictive prophecy is found mostly in the futurist and historicist approaches.

This section has provided an overview of the generically prophetic nature of the book of Revelation. The most powerful indicators put forth by supporters of this view are: a) the claims made by the book itself of being prophecy, b) the association of John with other prophets, making him one of them, and c) the use of Old Testament prophetic elements such as call/commission narrative and messenger formula.

## 'He made it known ... to his servant John': The authorship debate

The question of authorship of biblical books is one of the most contentious issues in biblical interpretation. The general public takes it for granted that most of the books bear the name of their author or contain specific evidence in the text itself allowing for precise identification of the person responsible for each work. However, it is not so. Many books of the Bible are anonymous. For example, the four Gospels of Matthew, Mark, Luke and John were anonymous compositions. The names given to them come from a traditional reference in the second century. The debate about authorship has been closely linked to the question of authority and canonicity, especially with the New Testament. These documents are considered to be authoritative because they presumably stemmed from people who were either eyewitnesses to Jesus' ministry or in direct contact with Jesus' closest associates. Many Christians tend to forget that the authority of the biblical works resides first in the belief that they were inspired by God and that they were accepted by the first Christian community as reflecting its faith. When trying to identify who the writer of the book of Revelation was, we will have to address two distinct types of evidence, internal and external.

### Internal evidence

The expression 'internal evidence' refers to information provided by the text itself. When looking at Revelation, the information we can gather relating to its author is quite sparse. This is what we can glean from the book:

### a) The name of the author was John

The author introduces himself four times in his composition (1.1, 4, 9; 22.8). However, there is no further designation of which John it is we are here encountering. The text does not say that he was an apostle, nor that he was the son of Zebedee nor that he had any first-hand knowledge of Jesus' ministry. The name itself is a grecized form of the Hebrew *Yohanan*, meaning 'God is gracious'. The name was fairly common among Jewish people. This led some commentators to suggest, as possible authors, the names of John the Baptist, John Mark of the book of Acts and John the Elder, in addition to that of John the apostle, one of the Twelve.

### b) The author identified himself as a prophet

As was presented in the previous chapter, the book of Revelation was referred to as a prophecy and John was linked to other prophets. Since he addressed seven different communities in Asia, it seems that the author was a wandering prophet.

### c) The author was probably a Palestinian Jew

The extensive allusions made to the Old Testament books, as well as the strong Semitic flavour of the Greek text of Revelation, suggest that the writer was not a native speaker of Greek. His writing sometimes reads like a translation from Aramaic or something overly influenced by Septuagint Greek, even maybe a conscious imitation of biblical Hebrew syntax. The author had knowledge of the Jerusalem temple, some of the worshipping activity that took place in it, as well as of the geography of Palestine (Armageddon). The apocalyptic genre contained in the book was also more typical of Palestinian Judaism. Some have speculated that he might have been a refugee from the First Jewish War, AD 66–70, which saw the destruction of the Jerusalem temple as well as the flight of many Jews from Palestine.

### External evidence

The epithet external refers to information which cannot be found in the text of Revelation itself, but comes mostly from Christian tradition. Traditionally speaking, the opinion has been very much in favour of identifying the author of Revelation with John, the son of Zebedee, the brother of James, one of the Twelve. The earliest testimony we have to this effect comes from a Christian theologian of the second century, Justin Martyr. In one of his works called *Dialogue with Trypho*, c. 155, Justin stated that:

There was a certain man with us, whose name was John, one of the apostles of Christ, who prophesied, by a revelation that was made to him, that those who believe in our Christ, would dwell a thousand years in Jerusalem; and that thereafter the general and in short, the eternal resurrection and judgement of all men would likewise take place. (Aune, 1997, p. li)

This opinion was shared by most Christian bishops and commentators of the time. The first serious challenge to this view came from bishop Dionysius of Alexandria (died *c.* 265). Dionysius became weary of a group of Christians whose leader, Nepos, had advocated a very literal, sensual, interpretation of the millennium passage found in Revelation 20. In order to steal Nepos' fire, Dionysius set his mind on trying to prove that the Apocalypse had not been written by John the Apostle, and should therefore not serve as a guideline for authoritative teaching. On the basis mostly of vocabulary and style comparison with the gospel and the three letters of John, he concluded that Revelation had nothing in common with these writings. The great church historian Eusebius of Caesarea accepted Dionysius' opinion and identified the author as a certain John the Elder who was mentioned in the writings of an earlier Christian theologian by the name of Papias of Hierapolis. However, the main Christian tradition has steadfastly reiterated that John the Apostle was the author of the book of Revelation.

A definitive consensus still has not been reached today. Internal evidence is favoured by some while others cling to the external. Conservative scholars emphasize the similarities in vocabulary between Revelation and the Johannine works (Gospel plus 1, 2, and 3 John) (Thomas, Mounce, Smalley). Most non-Evangelicals tend to favour a non-Johannine authorship for the book of Revelation (Charles, Boring, Ford, Aune, Roloff, Yarbro Collins, Wall, Krodel). In addition to Dionysius' analysis, this latter group of scholars add Christology, the Church, and eschatology as topics on which Revelation and the Johannine works differ. Others remain neutral in the identification of the writer, not really emphasizing the traditional view nor trying to disprove it either (Caird, Johnson, Beale). It is to be remembered that many a contemporary discussion of the authorship of the book of Revelation is guided as much by theological presuppositions and considerations (inerrancy, apostolic authority) as by historical ones. G. B. Caird, in his commentary on Revelation, put forth a point which should be pondered upon by anyone who becomes obsessed by the question of the authorship of the Apocalypse:

It would be interesting to have our curiosity on this point satisfied once and for all, but nothing more than curiosity is involved. The apostles were eyewitnesses of the ministry of Jesus, and in matters of historic fact their authority was of supreme importance. But the authority of a prophetic vision lies wholly in its content. The little that we know of the apostle John would add nothing to our ability to interpret the Revelation, and its authority would be neither increased if his authorship of it could be proved nor diminished if it were disproved. (1966, p. 4)

# 'John to the seven churches that are in Asia': Life-setting and letters

One of the striking features of the book of Revelation is its use of the letter format. When reading the first three chapters of the book, the reader usually realizes that this communication seems to be addressed to a number of very specific Christian communities. Who were these churches? What was John's link to them? What role does the epistolary genre play in the book of Revelation and how does it interact with the apocalyptic and prophetic ones examined earlier. Before answering these questions, the related issues of the dating and locale of Revelation's writing will be addressed.

## Date and location of Revelation

Two major hypotheses have been offered in regard to the dating of the book of Revelation. The first one sees it as having been written toward the end of Domitian's reign. Domitian was Roman emperor between 81–96. Revelation is, in this view, considered to have been penned around 95. The second major opinion sees the book as stemming from the era of Nero, who was emperor between 54–68. The debate is still going on but the former view has the upper hand right now among commentators and scholars. Let us examine some of the evidence which supports these two assessments.

As we saw in our survey of the authorship of Revelation, external evidence is information which is not taken strictly from the text itself, but from Christian tradition. The earliest external evidence we have on the question of the dating of Revelation comes from bishop Irenaeus of Lyons, writing around 180, who said that Revelation was beheld by John toward the end of the reign of Domitian. This testimony in favour of the later dating was upheld by the majority of Christian commentators. However, the best indicators for a possible date are found in the text of Revelation itself. By comparing these with the historical and archaeological knowledge that we possess of the Roman empire and the churches in Asia, we can at least establish some high probabilities.

First of all, the background of the book seems to be that of persecution, experienced or/and expected, as well as of divided allegiance. The author himself had been exiled to the island of Patmos because of his witnessing to God's word (1.9). The church of Pergamum counted at least one believer who was martyred (2.13). The believers in the church of Smyrna were being forewarned of the possibility that they might have to face a martyr's death. If persecution was in the air, which period of Christianity's history would meet the criterion of widespread persecution? The proponents of an early dating suggest that the persecution of Christians by Nero Caesar between 64–68 would be a good candidate. However, this same persecution was localized, and therefore affected only the Christians living in Rome, not those living in the rest of the empire. The persecution expected by the writer of Revelation seemed more widespread.

The other good candidate would be Domitian's period. It is very much argued today that Domitian did not engage in an empire-wide persecution of Christians. However, he did do some political cleaning toward the end of his reign and might have used the accusation of *atheism*, not being faithful to the gods of Rome, to get rid of some politically influential Christians, maybe even his own niece Domitilla. Most persecutions of Christians, up to that of Decius in 250, were probably local and of brief duration. Some scholars today doubt the existence of any persecution during the time of Domitian but point to the presence, at various levels, of general public hostility or social pressure which might have forced local or regional authorities to act against a small number of Christians (Yarbro Collins, Schüssler Fiorenza, Thompson). Others deny the presence of persecution completely (Knight). Therefore, the concept of persecution in itself, expected, imminent, or actual, is not enough to secure the dating of Revelation.

A major piece of evidence in favour of the later dating is the use of the symbolic name 'Babylon' to designate Rome (14.6; 16.19; 17.4; 18.2, 10, 21). These two empires were linked because they had in common the destruction of Jerusalem and its temple. This association became popular only after the Roman destruction of Jerusalem in AD 70. Another association is that of the beast, described in 13.3 and 17.8–11, with a legend that circulated in the Roman empire about Nero coming back from the dead. After he committed suicide in 68, rumours started circulating that he was not really dead (compare with the Hitler and Elvis legends) and that he would come back to retake the Roman empire.

Evidence for a dating during the Domitianic period is also gathered from the situation of some of the churches addressed in Revelation.

The churches at Ephesus, Sardis and Laodicea are accused of having lost their zeal for the faith and grown cold. A significant period of time would have been needed for such a spiritual deterioration to occur; especially in Ephesus, one of Paul's jewels. The church at Laodicea is also characterized as rich and lacking nothing (3.17). It is however known from archaeology that this city was almost completely destroyed by a violent earthquake in 60–61. The amount of time needed to rebuild it and bring it back to the status of wealthy would require a late dating of Revelation. All in all, the scale of scholarly opinion leans more toward a late dating than an earlier one.

The question of where John was when he wrote Revelation is not much contested. John himself stated in 1.9 that he was on the island of Patmos. Patmos, now called Patino, is a small island in the Aegean sea, part of a group of islands known as the Sporades. It was located not too far from the cities of Ephesus and Miletus. Patmos seems to have been used as a place of deportation for people who ended up on the wrong side of the provincial authorities. John specifies that he was there 'because of the Word of God and the testimony of Jesus', i.e., his Christian faith and most likely the refusal to worship the emperor. The use of the specific Greek past tense translated 'I was' might suggest that John had been on Patmos when he received the visions, but was somewhere else, probably Ephesus, when he actually wrote them down. Aune presents four possibilities why John might have been present on Patmos: (1) voluntary exile in lieu of the death penalty; (2) deportation with loss of rights and possessions; (3) temporary or permanent banishment without loss of property or rights; (4) interdiction to be in his home territory (1997, see pp. 79–80). No matter the official reason, John interpreted it as retaliation because of his faith. The island of Patmos and its shrine dedicated to the seer of Revelation can still be visited today.

## Revelation's audience

Revelation 1.4 presents John as addressing seven churches which are in Asia. Revelation 1.11 specifies the location of these communities: Ephesus, Smyrna, Pergamum, Thyatira, Sardis, Philadelphia and Laodicea. These were located in the Roman province of Asia, modern Turkey. A number of problems seemed to be afflicting these communities. For some, namely Ephesus, Sardis and Laodicea, John perceived that the spiritual enthusiasm which characterized their coming to Christ had slowly vanished. John reminded them of their former zeal and invited them to rekindle the fire of their faith. The churches of Smyrna and Philadelphia were having difficulties with

Jewish opponents (2.9; 3.9). The church in Thyatira was home base to a prophetess and her followers, opponents of John (2.20). A group called Nicolaitans, Christians who seemed to compromise with pagan society, was affecting the churches at Ephesus and Pergamum (2.6, 15).

Most of all, a sense of the inevitability of persecution was in the air, permeating most of John's direct address to these seven congregations. Therefore, John had to deal simultaneously with the problems of possible persecution, emperor worship, behavioural bargaining with pagan ways of life, influence of false prophets, as well as pressure from anonymous Jewish groups. His answer to all of these predicaments came in the form of a circular letter.

## Letters and epistolary framework

Scholars have long recognized that the book of Revelation contains a framework very reminiscent of the Pauline letters. It has been suggested that, at the time of the writing of Revelation, Paul's letters were circulating among Christian communities and would have influenced the author of Revelation. It is true that Revelation shares common features with the letter form used by Paul. However, these commonalties are probably based more on the use of a common model than on direct Pauline influence. Scholars are divided as to the role played by the epistolary genre within the book of Revelation. Most commentators consider it as merely a framework, subordinated to the main genre of apocalypse or prophecy (Beale, Aune, Mounce, Thomas, Yarbro Collins). Others see the whole book as a letter in which the author used prophetic and apocalyptic ways of expressing the content (e.g. Krodel, Roloff, Schüssler Fiorenza, Boring). The use of the letter format would have made it easy for Revelation to be read during worship assemblies. The beatitude in 1.3 and the liturgical formulas in 22.17, 20b suggest that it was read in such a setting.

Letters were very common in the ancient world. Their content varied as much as the ordinary e-mail message of our time. Letters were occasional literature. By occasional it is meant that the writer was addressing a particular situation. John's work seems to meet this criterion. He wrote to very specific groups of people who lived in a distinct region of the Roman empire. Chapters 2 – 3 provide us with seven different communications to as many Christian congregations. John assessed the health of each group and provided exhortation, encouragement, as well as promises of reward or punishment.

The study of Greek letters, and of Paul's particularly, has allowed biblical scholars to discern a basic epistolary format which included fixed elements. The typical letter included four parts: opening formula, thanksgiving, body or message, and a concluding formula. We can try to assess if John's own letter answers to this scheme. The opening formula consisted of three different elements: sender, addressee, greeting. If we look at 1.4–5a, we find these three elements:

> John [sender] to the seven churches that are in Asia [addressee]: Grace to you and peace from him who is and who was and who is to come, and from the seven spirits who are before his throne, and from Jesus Christ, the faithful witness, the firstborn of the dead, and the ruler of the kings of the earth [greeting].

The first epistolary element is thus well represented. One thing to remark is that the sender does not add to his name any title or descriptor. The writer John seems to have been a very well-known figure in the churches he addressed. The second element, thanksgiving, was replaced by a doxology (1.5b–6), as in some of Paul's letters. The third part was the body of the letter, everything that stood in between the thanksgiving and the concluding formula. For Revelation that would include everything from 1.9 to 22.17. The last verse of Revelation is typical of the concluding formula found in Paul's letters.

Proponents of the letter character of Revelation do have many elements to support their view. Most of all, the incessant debate as to whether Revelation is prophecy or apocalypse has given rise to a compromise which affirms that it is a prophetic-apocalyptic circular letter. The last word about the genre of Revelation should be that none of the three types, apocalypse, prophecy, letter, should be discarded. If they are present, it is probably because John intended them to help convey his message. Readers should respect this aspect of his work.

## Seven letters, seals, trumpets, and bowls: Structure in Revelation

For many written works, the question of structure is either obvious or easily agreed upon. One can consult a variety of commentaries on the Gospel of Luke and encounter a wide agreement as to its basic organization. When looking at modern books, one only needs to turn to the table of contents to glance quickly at the overall structure. It is therefore expected that some organizational pattern must underlie the book of Revelation. However, in the history of biblical scholarship, not one book has offered such an elusive structure as the book of Revelation. An examination of the numerous suggestions offered to date would easily fill a complete volume in this series. Why is Revelation's structure so hard to identify? How do we proceed in the search for such a foundational element?

## Structure in the eye of the beholder

As beauty lies in the eye of the beholder, so it seems to go with the structure of the book of Revelation. There tends to exist as many proposals as the number of writers who have tackled this task. Such a state of affairs might be surprising to the general reader. How can it be that people cannot agree on the way the book is organized? On some points, there is agreement. All would agree that the book holds a beginning, a middle, and an end. The delimitation of the beginning and the end of the book are fairly consistent among the majority of interpreters. The debate takes place mainly over the middle part of the book, usually from 4.1 to somewhere in chapter 22. When looking at these proposals, it is possible to classify them as sevenfold, chiastic, or bipartite, meaning divided in two parts.

Writers who offer sevenfold, chiastic, or bipartite schemes will pay attention to what they can actually identify within the text. This is closely related to the assumption that the writer John actually had a specific structure in mind when he wrote his book. The goal is now to identify the elements in the text that would allow the reader to identify such a structure. The main components which are used by today's interpreters are numbers, repetitive sentences and recurring images.

## Numbers, motifs, and images as structural markers

A cursory reading quickly leads the reader to recognize that numerous repetitions or recurring features are present within the book of Revelation. Many of these have become the main foundational elements used in the various structures proposed for this work. A closer examination of these proposals is warranted.

### Structure and the number seven

The book of Revelation is replete with numbers which usually bear a symbolic meaning: three and a half, 666, 144,000, and most of all seven. The number seven is used in relation to different elements of the book: churches (1.4, 11, 20), spirits of God (1.4; 3.1; 4.5; 5.6), stars (1.16, 20; 2.1; 3.1), lampstands (1.12, 20; 2.1), seals (5.1, 5; 6.1), trumpets (8.2, 6, 13), bowls (15.7; 16.1; 17.1; 21.9), plagues (15.1, 6, 8; 21.9), etc. The omnipresence of that specific numeral has attracted the attention of scholars in their search for structural elements.

Some have suggested that seven, as used for the letters, seals, trumpets and bowls, represents the key to Revelation's structure. Adela Yarbro Collins (1976) is the most well-known proponent of a sevenfold structure. To the groups of seven already mentioned, she adds a group

of seven unnumbered visions found in 12.1 – 15.4 and another s•
group in 19.11 – 21.8. If it could be proven that the book was b•
around seven groups of seven, Revelation would then be exhibiting
perfect symbolic structure. The number seven, as structural element
the most prevalent pattern in the book of Revelation. The m•
question to be asked of the sevenfold structure is: 'If there are six
seven septets, why did the author mention only four of them?' T
groups of seven are deduced by the interpreter instead of be•
explicitly mentioned in the text. An external element is theref•
brought into a structure supposedly based on an internal marker.

## Two-part structure

Many proponents of the sevenfold structure just addressed simult•
eously emphasize the presence of two great divisions in the book
Revelation. The beginning of the second part is often located at 1•
due to its seeming independence from what precedes it. Another way
dividing the two parts is to consider part one as consisting of 1.4 – 3.
and part two as 4.1 – 22.5. The second part is then analysed for its o•
substructure. Division of the content of the visions in two great cycle•
sometimes based on the presence of the two scrolls, one in 5.1, and
other at 10.2. Another structural element that can be emphasized is
double commission that the writer of Revelation received. He
commissioned in 1.11 and in chapter 10. All of these components •
be used to divide Revelation in two great visionary units.

## Chiastic structure

A third major type of structure which has been applied to the book
Revelation is that of the chiastic model. This form of structure is ba•
on an ABC D C'B'A' pattern. The elements found in part A
answered to by those in A', B by B' and so forth. The central part of •
chiasm is considered to be the primary point of the message which •
writer tried to convey. A good representative of such an approach •
Elisabeth Schüssler Fiorenza, who suggested the following chia•
structure:

A.  1.1–8 Prologue and Epistolary Greeting
B.  1.9 – 3.22 Rhetorical Situation in the Cities of Asia
C.  4.1 – 9.21; 11.15-19 Opening the Sealed Scroll: Exodus Plagu•
D.  10.1 – 15.4 The Bitter-Sweet Scroll: 'War' against the Commur•
C'. 15.5 – 19.10 Exodus from the Oppression of Babylon/Rome
B'. 19.11 – 22.9 Liberation from Evil and God's World-City
A'. 22.10–21 Epilogue and Epistolary Frame
(See Schüssler Fiorenza, 1991, pp. 31–7).

She therefore concluded that the central part of Revelation's message had to do with the little scroll which John eats in chapter 10 and the following events linked to it. One advantage of such an approach is that it emphasizes the unity and tightness of the book. The difficulty with this structure is that some of the elements do not completely correspond to one another. Also, if John intentionally wanted this kind of structure to be identified by his *hearers*, he would have had to include extremely clear markers that could be picked up by the audience. This is not evident.

The variety of opinions concerning the structure of the book of Revelation is a direct testimony to the literary genius of the writer John. The question remains, did he or did he not intend to use a specific structure? If so, how do we get at it? The one very important point to remember, when identifying a certain structure in Revelation, is the fact that the book was read aloud to a congregation, not being studied as if it were a textbook. Therefore, any intended structure must have been able to be picked up by a group of people *listening* to Revelation's story, not putting it under the microscope of an analysis that would ignore the aural nature of the book.

## Seals, trumpets, and bowls: Recapitulation, linear development, or both?

Since the time of Victorinus of Pettau (d. 304), the first known Latin interpreter of Revelation, the presence of repetitions and parallels has fed the interpretive debate. The passages describing the seven seals, the seven trumpets, and the seven bowls have raised the issue of whether John intended his readers to interpret these events as being linear, i.e., following each other in a chronological fashion; or as representing the same events, what is today called recapitulation. Many interpreters have defended each option while others have tried to combine the best of the two. Still others have endeavoured to come up with a new model which would, according to them, make more sense of these problematic passages. The sections of Revelation involved in this debate are identified in the outline proposed in chapter 2 as the seven seals (6.1 – 8.5), the seven trumpets and the three woes (8.6 – 11.19), and the seven bowls-plagues (15.1 – 16.21).

### Linear development: Following the timeline

The first-time reader of Revelation tends to treat the book with the same kind of expectations brought to the reading of one of the four Gospels. What is expected is that, as for any normal narrative, there is going to be a beginning, a middle and an end. The passages involving the seals, trumpets and bowls are thus addressed in a very linear way. They are considered as following one another in a strict chronological order: the seven seals are open, the seven trumpets are blown, and then the seven bowls are emptied enacting the seven plagues. Two well-known interpreters of Revelation who have defended this approach are R. H. Charles, whose commentary published at the beginning of the twentieth century has become a classic, and David Aune. Anyone could contend that this is the most logical way of reading what seems to be a basic narrative work. Most of the other books of the Bible, Genesis, Exodus, Joshua, Samuel, Kings, the Gospels, Acts, are all read in this way, why should Revelation be any different? Interpreters who hold to a futurist approach to Revelation are usually favourable to this way of analysing the relationship between the septets.

Factors which tend to support the linear, sequential reading of these passages are the following:

a) The judgement rendered in each septet increases from one group to the other. The punishment enacted by the blowing of each trumpet affects only a part (1/3) of humanity, or other aspects of creation, while the calamities provoked by the seven bowls tend to be more inclusive.

b) The sequence of events as well as the content of each group differ.

c) The opening of the seventh seal in 8.1 seems to be linked in a causal fashion to the appearance of the angels and the trumpets given to them (8.2).

d) The passage found at 9.4, 'They were told not to damage the grass of the earth or any green growth or any tree, but only those people who do not have the seal of God on their foreheads', seems to presuppose that the sealing of the elect mentioned in 7.3 has already taken place.

e) The passage at 15.1, 'Then I saw another portent in heaven, great and amazing: seven angels with *seven plagues*, which are *the last* . . .', implies that other plagues, the seals and trumpets, would have already occurred.

These elements enable proponents of this theory to see the occurrences described by the seals, trumpets and bowls as a chronological, sequential unfolding of the narrative events. However, major difficulties presented by these same passages have given rise to competing interpretations.

## Recapitulation: The inevitable judgement

Another approach to the relationship between the seven seals, trumpets and bowls is known as recapitulation. Its origins go back to the Latin commentary of Victorinus of Pettau written around 258–60. While not using the word 'recapitulation' Victorinus outlined its central idea which was that one should not be looking for a chronological order in the Apocalypse. The seals, trumpets and bowls are all considered as presenting the same set of events, but from a different perspective, or in greater detail. This approach stresses that the final judgement will come, it is inevitable. This view is the one adopted mostly by idealists and a few futurist interpreters (Caird, Yarbro Collins, Krodel, Schüssler Fiorenza, Beale). It is to be noted that Schüssler Fiorenza, Krodel, and Boring see this recapitulative aspect of Revelation as being progressive, like an upward conical spiral. Things are revisited while being simultaneously intensified.

The first textual hint that recapitulation might be involved in the septets comes from a close examination of the sixth and seventh seals, the seventh trumpet, and the seventh bowl. The sixth seal, 6.12–17, seems to present the final judgement as happening, as being completed. Its description of a total cosmological destruction makes it hard for anything else to take place. The silence of the seventh seal is seen as a continuation of that scene, since in apocalyptic literature, a period of silence often referred to judgement. The seventh trumpet, 11.15–19, once again presents images of the judgement as being exacted, being final. The seventh bowl, 16.17–21, once more offers a picture of final judgement. The question asked of these passages is whether they represent three different final judgments, which would be an oxymoron, or different depictions of the same event.

The similarity in the structure and content of some of the septets has also convinced many that recapitulation must be present. When examining the sixth seal, sixth trumpet and sixth bowl, one recognizes that each is built according to a three-part structure and that they share a common theme, an assessment of the general condition of believers and non-believers just before the final judgement. Similarly, the fifth component of each septet deals with the question of social justice. Proponents of the recapitulation theory emphasize that the events described in the septets cannot represent a linear development since the development is often interrupted by elements which do not fit in the flow of the story. These same intercalations have been analysed as either playing the role of hinges, joining two separate units that do not follow one another logically, or being part of the sandwich technique used by John. Even proponents of a linear theory acknowledge that some elements hinder the logical chronological development and have to be explained in some way (Thomas, 1995, pp. 540–41).

Critics of this approach have pointed to the fact that recapitulation does not account for the increase in severity of the chastisements presented in each septet. Even more, the fact that the three series of seven end in the same way does not mean that they all have to begin at the same time. Three sequences can start at different times but end at the same point, only their time span will differ, not their point of termination. While offering some enlightening insights, recapitulation, like linear development, suffers from some shortcomings.

## The telescopic theory: Dovetailing in the septets

In the past ten years, a new theory has been proposed as a way of keeping the linear development of the septets intact while allowing for some form of recapitulation, mostly in the intercalations. This scheme is known as the telescopic or dovetailing approach. This view 'sees the seventh seal as containing the seven trumpets and the seventh trumpet as containing the seven bowls' (Thomas, 1995, p. 531). This approach takes its cue from the fact that after the seventh seal has been broken, no judgement is enacted on earth-dwellers. This situation repeats itself with the seventh trumpet. Nothing happens after it is blown. The third woe is also considered in this view as being unfulfilled, unless it is similar to the seventh trumpet which includes all the seven plagues. The dovetailing theory can also explain the intensification of the punishments from the seven seals to the trumpets and the bowls. This approach thus emphasizes the progressive nature of the events described by the three septets of the seals, trumpets and bowls.

The three approaches outlined in this section can all be supported using the text of Revelation. This might be the reason why recent commentaries have been at odds over the presence and role of recapitulation within the septets (Aune versus Beale). It is to be remembered that the position adopted by the interpreters in regard to the septets is often dependent on their overall approach to the book of Revelation. An idealist or preterist will emphasize recapitulation while a strict historicist or futurist will favour linear development. A new branch of futurist interpretation has started turning to the telescopic approach in order to make sense of the progression in the book of Revelation as well as accounting for a minor role played by recapitulation. No doubt that this issue will remain a dominant one in the upcoming works on the Apocalypse of John.

# The four horsemen and 666:
# Revelation and symbolism

And I saw a beast rising out of the sea, having ten horns and seven heads; and on its horns were ten diadems, and on its heads were blasphemous names. And the beast that I saw was like a leopard, its feet were like a bear's, and its mouth was like a lion's mouth ... and I saw a woman sitting on a scarlet beast that was full of blasphemous names, and it had seven heads and ten horns. The woman was clothed in purple and scarlet, and adorned with gold and jewels and pearls, holding in her hand a golden cup full of abominations and the impurities of her fornication, (Rev 13.1–2; 17.3b–5)

When reading the book of Revelation, one cannot but be amazed, shocked, troubled and dismayed at the variety of fascinating, sometimes grotesque, violent, and even disgusting images which assault the reader in its every chapter. The dizzying array of symbols, metaphors and depictions which fill the pages of this work have inspired terror and awe among myriads of Christians throughout history. Martin Luther simply could not figure out what this was all about and came to the conclusion that this book did not teach Christ.

What does it all mean? How does one make sense of images such as those presented above? Are they to be taken literally? If not, how extensively should the non-literal interpretation be applied? These questions are still very much debated among Christian faithful who are trying to interpret the book of the Apocalypse. It is recognized by the majority of scholars that the book is replete with symbols. Disagreements appear over the nature of these symbols and the way in which they function. It is therefore important first to examine these two points before addressing the actual interpretation of a few symbols found in Revelation.

## The nature and use of symbolic language

The role of human communication is basically to allow one to form a mental structure of one's environment and to convey thoughts and ideas to others. Sounds are put together so as to represent a certain object as well as its characteristics. When needing to describe realities that are not material and concrete, such as emotions or spiritual concepts, human language must proceed at a different level than it usually does. This level is often referred to as the symbolic one. But what is a symbol and how is it used?

The word 'symbol' is derived from the Greek verb *symballein*, meaning to 'throw together': 'To think symbolically means to take something tangible ... like fire, and throw it together with something that has no material, physical form – like an emotion or a concept or an idea' (Stoutzenberger, 1993, p. 25). The symbol therefore allows one to get a grasp of something which cannot usually be experienced through the use of the senses. Symbolic language helps to express the reality of something which might be beyond the boundaries of sensory experience. In John's case, it enabled him to paint tableaux of the visions he had contemplated. Symbolic language allowed him to transfer his visionary experience to the hearer.

People today tend to use the words 'sign' and 'symbol' interchangeably. Generally, a sign is anything that is used to represent or stand for something else. A distinction should be made however between a sign, sometimes referred to as a steno-symbol, a symbol with only one meaning, and the fuller, tensive symbol which is polyvalent and is never exhausted by just one meaning. An example of a sign, or steno-symbol, is a red light at an intersection. It has only one meaning (or is supposed to) which is to stop. Any other interpretation of that sign would lead to deadly chaos in any city. A tensive symbol, on the other hand, is never fully interpreted by only one meaning. It elicits different responses from the variety of individuals who interact with it. Fire and water are good examples of tensive symbols. They are found within various cultures and exhibit an extensive range of meaning.

A symbol can be cultural, linked to a particular time and place in history, or universal, having meaning independently of the historical context in which it is being used. When looking at Revelation, many divergences of opinion centre around the nature of John's images. Are they signs or symbols? If they are symbols, are they cultural or universal? The way in which a person approaches these images will generate a specific interpretation. People who see in Revelation a series of signs will interpret each of these images as representing only one thing. Related to this is the code theory which sees the images of Revelation as constituting a secret form of language that must be deciphered in order to find out the meaning of the image. The difficulty with this approach is that code is used to hide meaning while John's explicit goal is not to conceal, but to reveal, i.e., *apocalypsis*, to unveil, to reveal. Anyone favouring a code-like approach seems therefore to be going against the grain of authorial intent.

A simpler approach is to take the images literally. Readers who favour this interpretation expect that what is described in Revelation is going to happen exactly as it is described in the book. Therefore, there will be a beast with seven heads and ten horns, and one like a Son of Man with a sharp two-edged sword coming out of his mouth, and breastplate-wearing locusts with faces like human faces, hair like women's hair, and teeth like lions' teeth. Some questions of logic arise when trying to figure out how to distribute ten horns on seven heads or how anyone can speak with a sword coming out of his mouth. This leads us to another aspect of the debate surrounding the use of symbols by John. To what extent are they to be interpreted symbolically or taken literally?

Arguing on the basis of the visionary experience of John, some interpreters hold to a full symbolic interpretation (Boring, Beale, Aune, Rowland). They also argue that if one part is to be interpreted symbolically, then the whole should be too. Proponents of the literal approach, however, insist that only passages explicitly asking for a symbolic interpretation should be dealt with in this way (Thomas, 1992, p. 35). The most proficient way to assess these different opinions is to investigate the meaning given to some of Revelation's most famous symbols.

## The four horsemen of the Apocalypse (Revelation 6.1–8)

Then I saw the Lamb open one of the seven seals, and I heard one of the four living creatures call out, as with a voice of thunder, 'Come!' I looked, and there was a white horse! Its rider had a bow; a crown was given to him, and he came out conquering and to conquer. When he opened the second seal, I heard the second living creature call out, 'Come!' And out came another horse, bright red; its rider was permitted to take peace from the earth, so that people would slaughter one another; and he was given a great sword. When he opened the third seal, I heard the third living creature call out, 'Come!' I looked, and there was a black horse! Its rider held a pair of scales in his hand, and I heard what seemed to be a voice in the midst of the four living creatures saying, 'A quart of wheat for a day's pay, and three quarts of barley for a day's pay, but do not damage the olive oil and the wine!' When he opened the fourth seal, I heard the voice of the fourth living creature call out, 'Come!' I looked and there was a pale green horse! Its rider's name was Death, and Hades followed with him; they were given authority over a fourth of the earth, to kill with sword, famine, and pestilence, and by the wild animals of the earth.

The first symbol we will study belongs to one of the most famous images of the book of Revelation. The four horsemen of the Apocalypse have fed the imagination of painters, poets, writers, and musicians, for hundreds of years. This image has become a powerful symbol of dread and doom. This study will not be an exhaustive one. However, specific elements will be analysed and the various interpretations attached to them will be presented. Meanings or applications that are central to a specific interpretive approach, preterist, futurist, historicist or idealist, will be highlighted along the way. Very often the different approaches agree on the meaning of a specific symbol. The differences appear in regard to the application made of that same symbol.

The four horsemen are part of the seven seals broken by the Lamb. This vision is linked directly to passages found in the book of the prophet Zechariah 1.8; 6.1–8. John alluded to these passages but transformed their meaning. As the first seal is broken, one of the four living creatures calls out 'Come!' and then 'there was a white horse! Its rider had a bow; a crown was given to him, and he came out conquering and to conquer' (6.2). The first point of interpretation is the colour of the horse. In the book of Revelation, white is usually the colour of righteousness, holiness and divine origin. It can also be considered as representative of conquest and victory. An interpretation, linked to Irenaeus' identification of the rider as being Christ, sees the white horse as representing the victorious progress of the gospel.

Identifying the rider of the white horse is a complicated task. As previously stated, the rider on the white horse has sometimes been identified as Christ. This point of view is based on similarities with the image of the victorious Christ found in Revelation 19.11. There also, Christ is riding a white horse and is conquering. Some interpreters stressed this identification (Alford, Ladd, Hendricksen). They supported this interpretation by using Mark 13.10 and Matthew 24.14. Both of these passages emphasize that the good news must be preached to all nations before the end comes. However, this identification has been severely contested. In 6.2, the rider has a bow and wears a wreath. In 19.11, however, he wears many crowns and a sword comes out of his mouth.

The similarities between the four horsemen have also convinced many that the first rider could not be Christ. Since the last three riders are evil, the first one must be evil too. Furthermore, Christ cannot be simultaneously opening the seal and then riding the first horse. If this rider does not stand for warfare in general (Charles, Caird, Mounce, Roloff, Aune, Wall), he might be a symbolic representation of the false christs and messiahs which are depicted in Mark 13.5–6; Matthew 24.4–5; Luke 21.8 as the first woe bound to precede Jesus' parousia (Johnson, Beale). He might be a personification of 'counterfeit Christian forces of the future (that) will attain worldwide domination' (Thomas, 1992, p. 424).

Other interpreters insist that the rider must represent one of two groups. The first one would be the Romans who in 67 set out to conquer the city of Jerusalem (Gentry). Another group that might be represented by the white rider would be the Parthians. This nation was a feared foe of the Roman empire, constantly threatening its eastern border. The Parthians were the most famous archers of antiquity. The presence of the bow in the hand of the first horseman leads many preterists to emphasize this identification, especially since in 62 the Romans suffered a humiliating defeat at the hands of the Parthian king Vologeses (Krodel, Boring, Schüssler Fiorenza).

The second horse to be summoned is a red one. Its colour is symbolic of bloodshed and violence. Its rider is given a sword so as to take peace away from earth. The expression 'so that people would slaughter one another' (6.4) might refer to civil war as well as global conflict. In a preterist vein, this symbol can be applied to the in-fighting and cannibalism which took place during the first Jewish revolt of 66–70, as well as the social unrest present in the Roman empire after the suicide of Nero Caesar in 68, and the rapid deaths of emperors Otho, Galba and Vitellius, all in a single year. Many scholars consider that the peace taken away from earth might be an ironic reference to the *Pax Romana*, the Roman peace which had been implemented by Caesar Augustus (Krodel, Boring, Ford, Mounce, Roloff, Aune). Other scholars interpret the second rider as mainly representing bloodshed and civil war, (Johnson, Charles) or a part of the beginning of the birthpains preceding the Second Coming of Christ (Thomas).

The third horse to appear on the scene is black, the colour of grief and mourning. Its rider holds a balance scale. This device was made of a horizontal bar from which hung two plates. In one plate would be a weight and in the other the object to be weighed. This rider is almost unanimously identified as a personification of famine or scarcity. This interpretation is due to the statement made by the voice coming from the midst of the four creatures saying 'A quart of wheat for a day's pay, and three quarts of barley for a day's pay ...' (6.6a). This passage illustrates a time of extreme inflation. It would take an individual a whole day's pay in order to provide himself/herself with an amount of food good only for *one* day. It would then be extremely hard to provide for a whole family.

The situation is thus one of great scarcity but not complete famine. A general interpretation sees this famine as a consequence of the war and internal strife represented by the second rider (Beale, Johnson). A preterist interpretation points to the lack of food which afflicted the Jerusalemites during the Roman siege of 69–70 (Gentry). These occurrences were well documented by the Jewish historian Flavius Josephus and the Roman historians Tacitus and Suetonius. It could also highlight the scarcity of food as a consequence of imperial militaristic conquest and rule (Schüssler Fiorenza, Roloff, Boring). Futurist interpreters see in this rider the coming of a great famine the likes of which has never been seen before (Thomas).

The last horse to come forth is designated by the Greek adjective *chlôros* which can be translated as green (as in the word 'chlorophyll'), yellowish-green, or a pale sickly green colour associated with corpses. The context seems to favour this last option. The rider of the horse is named Death. Strangely enough, this character is followed by another one whose name is Hades.

Hades was the Greek god of the underworld. In this passage, Hades seems to be a personification of the abode of the dead. His presence here has been interpreted in various ways. Hades' role has sometimes been considered as that of picking up the bodies behind Death, or as representing the kingdom of the underworld which is ruled by Death. Still others have seen the fourth rider and his companion as representing either a summary, a result, an intensification, or an epitome of the first three horsemen (Krodel, Mounce, Caird, Beale). This last conclusion has been countered by others who highlight the intensification of the punishments enacted by the four seals and maintain the individuality of the fourth horseman (Boring, Thomas).

Taken as a whole, the four horsemen of the Apocalypse are given a different theological interpretation by each of the four main approaches. The preterists see them as related to people who lived and events that occurred in Palestine and Asia during the first century. The futurists consider the four horsemen as representing specific future calamities which will take place before Christ's Second Coming. Historicists have not demonstrated any kind of consensus as to the identification of the four horsemen. Finally, idealists see the four riders as commonplaces in history, results of a fallen society permeated with evil and injustice.

### 666, the number of the beast (Revelation 13.18)

Throughout the history of Christianity, few numbers have fascinated believers more than the one found in Revelation 13.18. From Gregory Peck's discovery of Damian's tattooed head in *The Omen* to the rock group Iron Maiden's cover title, *The Number of the Beast*, the number 666 has stimulated endless representations within Western culture. The speculations surrounding the triple six have been unending. What is the significance of this symbol?

The first point of discussion concerning 666 is its context, Revelation 13.18: 'This calls for wisdom: let anyone with understanding *psêphisatô* the number of the beast, for it is *arithmos anthrôpou*. Its number is six hundred sixty-six.' The two expressions left in trans- literated Greek have been the object of many discussions among Revelation scholars. The first word is the verb *psêphisatô* which is related to the Greek word for pebble, *psêphos*. Pebbles were used by the ancients to count. The basic meaning of the verb seems to be that of calculating something out. Certain translations are not so literal and use words like 'reckoning' or 'figuring out' instead of calculating. These wish to emphasize the element of understanding without the presence of an actual link with any form of arithmetic.

The expression *arithmos anthrôpou* is even more of a problem since its translation usually mirrors the interpretative tendency of the translator. The word *arithmos* means number, and *anthrôpou* is the possessive form of the Greek word for man, or human being. As a whole, the expression can be translated in two ways. First, in a general way, as 'a human number' meaning not a spiritual or divine one, a number which can be understood without help from God or the heavenly realm. The second way of translating the expression is more definite as 'the number of a man', or 'the number of a person'. In this case, the symbol is thought to represent a very specific individual. The interpretation given to this number is often linked to the translation of these two key words.

Many interpreters favour the second translation. In their minds, there is no doubt that the number represented a very specific individual who lived before the fall of Jerusalem in AD 70: the Roman emperor Nero (Charles, Wall, Krodel, Aune, Bauckham, Roloff, Harrington). This identification is done through a process known as gematria, a term linked to the Greek word *geometria* meaning 'to measure with numbers'. Gematria was a form of play with words. In ancient Greek and Hebrew, there existed no numbers. Letters were assigned a numerical value dependent on their position in the alphabet. For example, the two Hebrew letters *'aleph* and *yôd* together would have represented the number eleven, since *'aleph* is the first letter of the Hebrew alphabet, with a value of one, and *yôd* was the tenth, with a corresponding value of ten. Other letters were assigned values in the tens and the hundreds. Using gematria one could write numbers which were actually the numerical representation of a word. Examples of this type of riddle have been found in the ruins of Pompeii. One of these said 'I love her whose number is 545 (ΦΜΕ)' (Deissmann, 1965, p. 276). Since many names could have the same total, it seems that the use of such a riddle presupposed that the reader of the graffito would already have known who was supposed to be represented by the number.

The Greek words for Nero Caesar, *qaisar nerôn*, when transliterated in Hebrew as *qsr nrwn*, amount to a total of 666. Interpreters emphasize that this fits well with the context of chapters 13 and 17 which speak symbolically of the Roman Empire in general and Nero in particular. The beast is therefore identified as the dissolute Roman leader who persecuted Christians and committed suicide in 68. Even though this has become the majority opinion among interpreters of Revelation, many are quick to point out the problems involved in such an interpretation.

The first weakness is that the spelling for the word Caesar is missing a letter. It was usually spelt *q'sr*. Spelt in the traditional way, the words *q'sr nrwn* would have totalled 676, not 666. The alternative spelling has been found in only one document among the Dead Sea Scrolls. Another difficulty is with the use of gematria. If accepted as such, this would be John's only use of this technique in his whole book. Of all the other numbers used in Revelation, none are said to require the use of gematria in order to be interpreted. They are taken as either completely literal or completely symbolic. Why gematria here?

Another point emphasized in refuting this approach is that, for the total to be reached, one has to take a Greek word and transliterate it in Hebrew. This is questionable since John was probably writing to an audience of native Greek speakers. Since he wrote to be understood on the first take, it stretches the imagination to affirm that a few bilingual members of the intended audiences would have been able to interpret the number for their fellow Christians. This would have required a complete interruption of the reading in progress, something quite unlikely in the liturgical context in which the book of Revelation would have been read aloud. Furthermore, if John had wanted this word to be understood in Hebrew, why did he not say so, as he specifically did in 9.11 and 16.16?

The next weakness of this interpretation is that many names could end up with the same total. How were the hearers supposed to home in on a specific emperor? By using the context? Maybe. Another puzzling element about this type of interpretation is that, if it were the correct one, none of the ancient theologians of the Church remembered it. Irenaeus of Lyons, who lived around 180, showed no knowledge of the identification with Nero. His solutions to the riddle were three different names. Furthermore, when transliterating a Greek word in Hebrew, many variations were possible. One of the most thorough investigations of the Neronic interpretation has been offered by Richard Bauckham who acknowledged the difficulties already mentioned and widened the context of the discussion to include a study of the influence of the *Nero redivivus* legend and Christian apocalyptic tradition (1993a, pp. 384–452).

Many scholars share Irenaeus of Lyons' emphasis that Christians should not indulge in endless speculations about the identity of the individual represented by this number (Thomas, Mounce). Most futurist interpreters stress that when this demonic leader appears on the scene of history, the number will *de facto* become clear to all who have understanding.

Historicist interpreters have had a field day with the interpretation of 666. The flights of fancy have sometimes stretched the limits of credibility. The number of the beast has been calculated as representing, among the many, several Roman emperors and popes, Martin Luther, Joseph Stalin, Adolph Hitler, Benito Mussolini, Ronald Reagan, and even Bill Gates of the famed Microsoft. The race is still on in this school of interpreters for a final, consensual, identification.

Another group of interpreters favours the first translation of *arithmos anthrôpou* presented previously and stresses that John's 666 should be interpreted more broadly or symbolically, as with all the numbers found throughout Revelation (Beale, Rowland, Johnson). In their opinion, to introduce a new form of interpretation at this point in the book is totally unwarranted. They would rather emphasize the symbolic meaning conveyed by the number. Since six is one short of the number representing completeness, which is seven, a triple six could symbolize complete imperfection, total failure to attain God status, 777. These interpreters have offered various meanings for 666, going from false religion, to godless society, to eternal failure, to the bestial nature of individuals who refuse God's lordship. Some of them point to the fact that the Greek word for beast, *thêrion*, when transliterated in Hebrew, equals 666. A specific name is therefore not to be sought under the number of the beast.

The debate surrounding the interpretation of the number found in Revelation 13.18 is still very much alive. In these times of renewed apocalyptic expectations, many individuals and groups who are awaiting the near consummation of history devote countless hours trying to identify the man or woman bearing the number of the Antichrist. The fascination which this numeral has exercised over countless Christians does not seem about to fade.

## Looking back

This chapter has offered some non-exhaustive information about the various themes which remain central to any interpretation of the book of Revelation. This was intended to help the reader of this *Introduction* get a better understanding of the various elements which constitute a great part of most commentaries. Revelation is a book which seems to defy our methods of interpretation. However, the four traditional methods of interpretation have recently been challenged by new kinds of approaches. The hope is that these might help further unravel the tapestry of meaning woven by the Seer of Patmos.

# 5

## Revelation and the New Interpretive Approaches

For nearly one hundred years, the predominant way of reading and interpreting the book of Revelation has been through the use of the historical-critical or the grammatico-historical method. These two approaches are known as diachronic methods. This means that they consider the meaning of the text to be recoverable through the study of its history, all the way back to its original author, his intent, the sources he used, as well as the 'setting in life' (*Sitz im Leben*) from which he wrote. The aim is to try and find what the writer intended to say to his original audience and how the text might have grown through certain editorial stages.

However, in the past thirty years, a new family of interpretive methods has been challenging the near monopoly held by these traditional methods. The newcomers all share one thing in common. They are synchronic instead of being diachronic. This means that they are more interested in what a text has to say to the reader in the form it possesses today, than in the historical knowledge that can be gained from digging for its historical background. Fresh interpretations of several books of the Bible have been offered. Some of these approaches have been mostly literary in character, while others have been more interested in the socio-political aspect of life.

In this chapter, we will survey some of these new methods and identify their contribution to the study of the book of Revelation. We will begin by addressing the question of whether the Bible is literature or not. This will be followed by the presentation of a literary approach to the Bible known as narrative criticism. Afterward, we will turn our attention to socio/political readings of Revelation as exemplified by feminist and liberation interpretations of the book of Revelation. The last section of the chapter will focus on intertextuality, an approach which aims at highlighting the tapestry of meaning created by different sources used by a given author. Intertextuality will allow us to examine the relationship between the book of Revelation and the Hebrew Scriptures.

## Revelation and literary criticism

Is the Bible literature? Can it be read and studied in the same way as Homer's *Odyssey* or Milton's *Paradise Lost*? Many believers would answer 'no' to these two questions, based on their understanding of its divine provenance and its unique character. Others would refuse due to their opinion that literature is always fictional. They would argue, therefore, that the Bible cannot be classified as literary since, in their opinion, it is historically factual. Many others, however, would contend that if Scripture was mediated by God through human authors, it was consequently bound to human ways of writing, thus, to known forms of literature.

Literature can be broadly defined as creative writing. For a work to be considered literary, it should be able to provide answers to the following questions:

1) Does it exhibit a specific genre?
2) Does it show and describe (imaging aspect) instead of just telling (expository aspect)?
3) What part of the human experience does it illustrate (life, death, love, hate, failure, success, etc.)?
4) Does it influence the reader (affective component)?
5) Does it use elements related to artistic form (pattern, theme, coherence, balance, etc.)?
6) Does it use forms of language which are literary (metaphors, similes, allegories, etc.)?
7) Does it use patterns of language which are literary (parallelisms, strophes, rhymes, etc.)?

All of the above questions can easily be applied to many books of the Bible, including the book of Revelation. The logical conclusion, then, is that the Bible is in fact a literary work. This confirms the possibility of studying Scriptures using the tools of literary criticism.

### Narrative criticism

The branch of literary criticism that specializes in the study of stories is called narrative criticism. Scholars who practice this discipline examine each text using elements which define the narrative or story genre. These individuals, when studying the Bible, are not primarily interested in Scriptures as representing a kind of theological textbook supplying

Christians with propositional truths, or as a history of ancient Israel. On the contrary, they look at the Bible as a collection of stories. They read the books of the Bible in the same way one would read J. R. R. Tolkien's *The Hobbit*. Narrative critics are not concerned with elements external to the text. They focus on the story and what it is saying. If we take for example the debate on the authorship of Revelation which was discussed in the previous chapter, the narrative critic would not be interested in who the historical author of the book was, but mainly in the image of himself he unconsciously projected in the text. This is known as the *implied author* or *author-in-the-text*. For example, when reading Revelation, one often encounters allusions to the Hebrew Scriptures. This allows the reader to build an image of the author as a Jewish Christian. The story must be related to the point of view of this author-in-the-text, not the historical one. Very often, however, the implied author closely resembles the historical one.

The same goes for the question of the audience of the book. Narrative critics state that what is important is not so much the historical individuals and groups who received the book of Revelation, but the image of the ideal reader that the writer had in mind when he wrote his book. This image of the perfect reader can be found by using the text itself. This is called the *implied reader* or *reader-in-the-text*. The example used above for the implied author can help us illustrate the idea of implied reader. When the writer of Revelation used his hundreds of allusions to the Hebrew Scriptures, he probably expected the reader to, almost automatically, make the connection with each passage from these same books. In reality, many of the original hearers/readers were probably incapable of performing this phenomenal task. This has serious implications for today's readers. First of all, it is a strong reminder that the book of Revelation was not written for us today. Second, it means that in order to read the story of Revelation for all it is worth, we need to try to become like the perfect reader that John had in mind. This requires quite an effort on the part of everyone who approaches this text.

In chapter 2, we studied the story of the book of Revelation. Many of the concepts used by narrative critics were presented at that time. Definitions offered in that chapter may be referred to, as needed, during the following discussion.

The book of Revelation, as story, includes a beginning, a middle and an end. In addition to that, it possesses the elements of plot, setting and characterization:

## Plot

The main plot of Revelation is the battle between good and evil, God and Satan. The story starts with the introduction of the main character and proceeds, through a series of events, to the resolution of the main problem, which is accomplished through the defeat of evil and the establishment of the New Jerusalem. Some readers might find the flow of the story difficult to follow. This is due to the fact that the story of Revelation is made up of episodes, smaller stories which make up the overall narrative. David Barr, a biblical scholar who performed a narrative analysis of Revelation, even came to the conclusion that Revelation was in fact three stories not one. He argued that Revelation presents the story of Jesus Christ in three different ways: The Letter Scroll (1.1 – 3.22), the Worship Scroll (4.1 – 11.18), and the War Scroll (11.19 – 22.21). These three blocks do not share a causal link; one story does not lead to the other. However, 'they gain their meaning by appearing together within the common frame of John's vision and letter' (1998, pp. 15–16).

## Setting

Revelation possesses various settings which at times are extremely stereotypical: Heaven is bright and high, while hell is dark and low, a bottomless pit. The action always happens somewhere. The settings form what is known as the story world. When studying Revelation as narrative, the reader must remain within the boundaries of the story world and abstain from bringing in elements from his/her own world which are external to the narrative.

## Characterization

As seen in chapter 2, Revelation possesses a variety of characters including Jesus as the protagonist, the hero; and Satan as the antagonist, the ultimate adversary. Close attention should be paid to the characters. By following their interactions with each other and with the different settings, as well as their role in plot development, the reading experience and the understanding of the whole story will be greatly enhanced.

It is therefore vital to concentrate on these elements when reading the story and use them in exactly the same way one would for, let us say, a novel. Another important thing to remember is that the book of Revelation conveys its message through imagery, symbolism. When reading the book of Revelation as story, the reader should not dissect the images and try to match a specific symbol with a particular element of reality. One must feel the power of the image, not reason it. Readers should feel the disgust inspired by the image of the harlot drunk with the blood of the saints, instead of trying to figure out who or what she represents. The text must be allowed to trigger the right side of the brain, which is the artistic, imaginative side. The description of the One like a Son of Man in Revelation 1.14–16 is a perfect example of such powerful imagery:

> His head and his hair were white as white wool, white as snow; his eyes were like a flame of fire, his feet were like burnished bronze, refined as in a furnace, and his voice was like the sound of many waters. In his right hand he held seven stars, and from his mouth came a sharp, two-edged sword, and his face was like the sun shining with full force.

The readers must refrain from trying to build a 'logical' image of this character because by doing so, they empty it of its evocative power. On the contrary, they should let themselves be transfixed by the burning gaze of his fiery eyes, be blinded by the reflection of the bronze feet, hear the deafening sound of his voice, and feel the scorching heat radiating from his face. This is what the image is all about; a sensory experience which triggers the readers' imagination and envelops them in the imagery of the story world. Read in this way, Revelation will impact the reader at a primal, deep-seated level which no exegetical commentary could ever reach. It is ironic that at a time when Western culture is driven by visual stimuli so many of us still have problems interacting with Revelation, Christ the conqueror's picture book.

The images of Revelation are archetypal. This means that they are universal, that they can be found in literature stemming from various cultures and different periods in history. Within Revelation we read about life, death, water, sun, darkness, all of which can be found in an innumerable number of stories. Leland Ryken has pointed out that Revelation is very similar to folk literature. He sees the last half of the book as being filled with images and motifs which are characteristic of stories everyone has read:

> a woman in distress who is marvelously delivered, a hero on a white horse who kills a dragon, a wicked prostitute who is finally exposed, the marriage of the triumphant hero to his bride, the celebration of the wedding with a feast, and the description of a palace glittering with jewels in which the hero and his bride live happily ever after. (1992, pp. 488–9)

These images are the stuff of dreams, of folk tales and children's stories which have spoken to humanity through the centuries. As human beings, we identify with stories because our own lives are stories. We have a beginning, a middle and an end. Many characters enter our existence, some to help us, others to oppose us. We move from setting to setting, overcoming obstacles so as to reach the end of our story and join the eternal divine narrative. This is why narrative criticism can be such a powerful way of reading Revelation. It lets the story talk to us with all its gore and glory, its eternal hope among seemingly endless despair, and its reward of eternal blessing for the ones who persevere. This is Christ's story begging to become part of our own.

## Revelation and socio-political criticism

In the past thirty-five years, theological movements known as 'liberation theologies' have taken the theological world by storm. Under this general label stand systems of thought such as feminist and womanist theologies, Latin American liberation theology, black theology and environmental theology. These movements have spawned their own way of reading and applying Holy Scriptures which sometimes differs radically from the traditional approaches. Two of them, Latin American liberation theology (LALT) and feminist theology, offer surprising new ways of interpreting the book of Revelation.

### Revelation and Latin American liberation theology

Latin American liberation theology was born out of the work of several individuals and groups. The most well-known advocates of this approach include Gustavo Gutiérrez, the 'father' of LALT, as well as Leonardo Boff, Juan Luis Segundo, and José Miguez Bonino.

In 1968, building on the momentum of the Second Vatican Council, the Conference of Latin American Catholic bishops, gathered at Medellín, shocked the Christian Church by radically applying the social teachings of the Church to the Latin American context. Their attacks on ecclesiastical officials, who were accused of cavorting with the ruling powers, as well as their description of 'institutionalized violence' against the poor, sounded the clarion call for this new theological movement. LALT stood theology on its head. Orthopraxy, correct action, was now considered as preceding orthodoxy, correct doctrine.

A second central presupposition became known as 'the preferential option for the poor'. The poor are the economically destitute, the ones who have nothing and lack everything; the ones who suffer due to structures of power which oppress them and transform them into nonpersons. This option was presented as more than a mere human choice. It was God's own: 'Preference for the poor means that even though God loves all people, he identifies with the poor, reveals himself to the poor and sides with the poor in a special way' (Grenz and Olson, 1992, p. 218). This divine favouring of the poor and the oppressed is considered as granting them an 'epistemological privilege', a head start in understanding God and his revelation. This privilege, when applied to the interpretation of Revelation, means that:

Those who do not know this suffering through oppression, who do not struggle together with God's people for the sake of the gospel, and who do not feel in their own bodies the meaning of oppression and the freedom and joy of fighting against it shall have great difficulty understanding this letter from Patmos. (Boesak, 1987, p. 38)

These theological presuppositions have led liberation theologians to read the book of Revelation in a radically different way than what had been offered, and is still being offered, by white, middle-class scholarship stemming from within the comfortable walls of academia more than from the poor's concerns. Latin American theologians tend to consider Revelation as a book which outlines a spirituality of resistance and offers direction as to how to build an alternative reality (Richard, 1995, p. 3). Catherine Keller adds that 'according to liberationist reading, Revelation belongs to an entire genre of resistance to colonization' (1996, p. 39). An example of LALT's way of reading Revelation can be illustrated through the use of Revelation 6.9–11 which depicts the plea of the martyrs:

When he opened the fifth seal, I saw under the altar the souls of those who had been slaughtered for the word of God and for the testimony they had given; they cried out with a loud voice, 'Sovereign Lord, holy and true, how long will it be before you judge and avenge our blood on the inhabitants of the earth?' They were each given a white robe and told to rest a little longer, until the number would be complete both of their fellow servants and of their brothers and sisters, who were soon to be killed as they themselves had been killed.

Liberation theology identifies these souls as those of the poor, the destitute, the landless who suffered at the hands of powerful landlords and corrupt governments backed by European and North American politico-economic interests. The document of the Puebla meeting of Latin American Catholic bishops, held in 1979, echoed this interpretation by stating that:

from the depths of the countries that make up Latin America a cry is rising to heaven, growing louder and more alarming all the time. It is the cry of a suffering people who demand justice, freedom, and respect for the basic rights of human beings and peoples. (In Arens Kuckerlkorn, Díaz Mateos and Kraft, 1998, p. 1859)

These martyrs, whose voices were silenced by hunger, disease and death squads, are identified by LALT as the ones crying out to God when the fifth seal is broken.

Read through the interpretive lens of LALT, Revelation's images become imbued with ultimate political and economic significance. Liberation theologians are interested in the historical background of the book as a way of allowing them to link these same images to the situation experienced by the masses in Latin American countries. The beast with seven heads and ten horns of Revelation 13 might have been Nero in the mind of the writer of the Apocalypse, but for liberation theologians it embodies all the institutions bent on treating the poor as nonentities, as slaves to the system, who can ultimately be ditched in a mass grave, never to be seen again.

The beast of the earth of Revelation 13.11–17, often referred to as the false prophet, might have represented the cultic apparatus of emperor worship in the first century. However, for the Latin American populace, this beast incarnates the propaganda machine used by dictatorial governments and repressive regimes to brainwash people and to silence any dissenting voice. The kings of the earth who have committed fornication with the great Harlot and the merchants of the earth who have grown rich from the power of her luxury (Rev 18.3) are easily identifiable for Latin American readers of Revelation. These images represent for them the European and North American governments, companies, and international conglomerates who ensure their own wealth by exploiting the cheap labour available in many Latin American countries. For these hearers of Revelation, it is not hard to identify who the followers of the Beast are and who wear its mark. Company logos hold quite a different meaning for the destitute of Ecuador, San Salvador or Nicaragua.

North American and European sensibilities often lead to a toning down of the political views espoused by the book of Revelation as well as of its violent, gory imagery. European and North American Christians do not feel comfortable with a Jesus who, instead of preaching non-retaliation, comes out to utterly destroy the enemies of God's people. Latin American Christians who have been starved to death, beaten up and tortured, who have witnessed the assassination of religious leaders and the disappearance of government critics, have lost these comfortable, middle-class sensibilities. The Christ they look up to is the glorious rider of the Apocalypse, the Lamb who leads the armies of God to complete victory. Having no power of their own, they feed from the promise made by Christ to those who endure and persevere. Pablo Richard, in his liberation-based commentary, stresses, however, that:

> The function of these texts is not to generate violence or hatred, but rather to express the situation of extreme oppression and suffering that the people of God are experiencing. The language of people living in dire want or under cruel persecution today is not very different. We cannot expect the poor to speak the refined diplomatic language of the powerful. (1995, p. 31)

The message of John which emphasized the impossibility of compromising with any atheist, anti-Christian, form of government strikes at the heart of the struggle experienced by multitudes of witnessing Christians in Latin America.

This is the powerful message of Revelation as understood and lived by those throngs of faithful followers of Christ whose plight gave rise to liberation theology. Their reading of Revelation is a powerful approach which should make every citizen of the oppressing countries, United States, England, Canada, etc., feel extremely uncomfortable. Europeans and North Americans (this writer included) who dare read Revelation through the eyes of the Latin American poor and their liberation perspective might end up realizing that instead of following the Lamb, they are actually more inclined to listen to the voice of the Lamb-like Beast. The (trade)mark they wear often reflects that choice.

## Revelation and feminist theology

Ever since the popular stirrings of the women's lib movement of the 1970s, feminist theology and feminist biblical criticism have been maturing and contributing fresh perspectives in the domains of Christian theology and biblical studies. Feminist theology seeks to rediscover the Christian experience of women, their contribution to the universal Church, as well as raise awareness of the oppressive patriarchal structures which make up the belief system and the organizational aspect of the Christian religion. Hard questions are asked: 'How can a woman interact with a God who is referred to as Father?' 'How can Christianity be delivered from a misogynist tradition which has legitimated violence and oppression against women for almost two thousand years?'

For its part, feminist biblical criticism aims at recovering the role of women in the biblical narratives, as well as trying to attract attention to the ways in which women are depicted there. The books of the Bible all stemmed from within a patriarchal culture. This expression denotes a form of society which centres around the males and treats females and children almost as nonentities. Feminist biblical critics also challenge the androcentrism which is not only part of Scriptures but also of the interpretive tradition which has developed since the second century. Androcentrism is the political, social, literary and religious bias which puts males at the centre of the universe, presenting this gender as the ultimate norm of being to whom everything and everyone else is subsumed. Feminist interpretation is more than just biblical interpretation, it is cultural critique. Feminist critics are suspicious of the biblical texts and their traditional interpretations since they tend to maintain the patriarchal and androcentric *status quo*.

When addressing the book of Revelation, feminist criticism concentrates on the gender issues present in the book, mainly 'the toxic misogyny of much of its imagery' and symbolism (Keller, 1996, p. 29). Many interpreters tend to sweep most of the gender implications of the text under the rug. This is done by saying that it was not the writer's intent or that the symbol itself is being misinterpreted. Feminist criticism is concerned however with the effects any reading of Revelation will have on an average reader who is mainly influenced by the surface meaning of the text.

An example of possible gender bias is found in Revelation 14.1, 4:

> Then I looked, and there was the Lamb, standing on Mount Zion! And with him were one hundred forty-four thousand who had his name and his Father's name written on their foreheads. It is these *who have not defiled themselves with women*, for they are virgins; these follow the Lamb wherever he goes. They have been redeemed from humankind as first fruits for God and the Lamb.

A first reading of this passage affirms that these 144,000 are with the Lamb because, among other things, they did not have sexual intercourse with women. Furthermore, the term used is 'defiled' an extremely negative, pejorative term. At first sight, this is a group of male ascetic celibates.

Interpreters, mostly men, are quick to point out that sexual immorality or adulterous intercourse can be a symbol for idolatry in the Bible, and that this passage is metaphorical. To counter such an interpretation, Catherine Keller states that:

> when a text goes to the length of adding a perfectly prosaic explication of the exclusive sexuality envisioned (as I cannot but read the phrase 'these who have not defiled themselves with women' to do), the excuse of metaphor no longer applies. (1996, pp. 524–25, parentheses are hers)

Furthermore, in this case, the passage does not talk about sexual immorality or prostitution, but only about sexual contact including that which could have been done even within the boundaries of marriage. That is why, even if this passage is considered as presenting a group of elect, men and women, who did not compromise themselves with idolatry, feminist critics still see in it an overt condemnation of sexual contact with women. To say that this symbolic group includes women would make for an extremely strange use of the image on the part of the writer John. Why would John have intended to include women in a group that is presented as 'not having defiled themselves with *women*'? He might just as well have meant to present a group of select eunuch warriors who dedicated themselves completely to the Lamb.

Another strongly negative feminine image used in the book of Revelation is that of the Great Harlot. What some feminist critics feel uncomfortable with is that, in the end, she is raped and killed in an excessively brutal way, all with the assent of God. Tina Pippin, a feminist writer, has questioned the significance of having one of Revelation's greatest emotional climaxes, where the reader's frustration and fear can finally be released, coincide with the killing of a woman who is made to stand and fall as the symbol of an oppressive political power. The Harlot gets what she deserved and the reader feels good about it. In regard to this passage, Pippin concludes that 'The object of desire is made the object of death. The Whore/Goddess/Queen/ Babylon is murdered (a sexual murder) and eaten and burned. This grotesquely exaggerated vision of death and desire accentuates the hatred of the imperial power – and of women' (1992, p. 58). She wonders what would the readers' reaction be if this was a male prostitute being raped and murdered. 'Would this symbol then be acceptable if the violence was imposed on a male? I think that the gang rape and murder of a male would be totally unacceptable to biblical scholars and the "symbolism" of the evil empire would break down at this point' (Pippin, 1999, p. 94). In regard to the same image, Catherine Keller inquires 'Why this trope to depict the defeat of the oppressor? In God's name, a powerful, sexual, bejeweled woman is stripped, humiliated, and devoured by hairy and horny beasts. Vision becomes voyeurism: a pious snuff picture unfolds' (1996, p. 76).

The image of the whore had previously been used by John in his letter to the church at Thyatira where a prophetess opposed him. Instead of dealing with her fairly, John resorted to insults and possible veiled threats of violence against her. The prophetess was pejoratively called Jezebel. Jezebel, as portrayed in the two Books of Kings, was the non-Israelite wife of King Ahab of Israel. She had hundreds of prophets of Yahweh slaughtered and became the sworn enemy of the prophet Elijah. Her life ended when she was thrown out the window of her palace (by a man) and most of her dead body was devoured by the dogs. For John to call this prophetess Jezebel might have been more than mere name calling. Adela Yarbro Collins adds that 'John's name-calling has obscured the fact that we have here an important indication of the leadership of women in the early church of this region' (1998, p. 405).

However, the feminine is not only represented as negative and powerless in the book of Revelation. Many feminist critics want to emphasize the strong, positive, images of women found there. One of these positive images is found in Revelation 12.1, '. . . a woman clothed with the sun, with the moon under her feet, and on her head a crown of twelve stars'. This woman gives birth to a son who will be the one to defeat the Dragon. She is represented with all the attributes of a goddess, maybe Leto who gave birth to Apollo, who in turn destroyed the dragon Python. This female character is most probably an image of the chosen community from which the Messiah came forth. Even if her presence is short lived within the narrative, it is one of the most powerful ones.

Another positive feminine character in the book of Revelation is the Bride of the Lamb, the New Jerusalem. She is the ultimate place of rest for the faithful and the eternal dwelling of God. However, some feminist critics are not completely satisfied with a positive interpretation of this symbol since, like the rest of the Bible, it portrays women in a restrictive manner. Women are either virgins, wives, mothers or harlots. The virgin is the one whose sexual activity is non-existent and under complete patriarchal control. Her polar opposite, the harlot, uses her sexuality as she wishes, independent of male control, and is therefore a constant threat. In this case, the Bride is under the control of the Lamb. The repertoire of feminine roles in Revelation is overall quite limited.

A feminist interpretation of Revelation first emphasizes the danger of reading the book as a divine acceptance of violence toward women, as illustrated in the passages relating to the Harlot. The next step consists in a rehabilitation of the positive feminine characters of the book. This goes for the prophetess of Thyatira who was strong enough and influential enough to become a serious opponent to a male leader; as well as for the woman clothed with the sun and her ally the goddess Gaia, Mother Earth, who protected her from the flood attack of the Dragon (Rev 12.15–16). All of this is included in a larger cultural critique aimed at establishing true relationships of complete equality between men and women as willed by Christ.

## Revelation and the Old Testament: Source-criticism and intertextuality

Readers of the book of Revelation might often get the funny feeling that they have read some of its passages somewhere before. This feeling might even lead some to try and identify the references used by the writer of the Apocalypse. Such a search would undoubtedly reveal John's use of many works found in the Old Testament, especially the books of Daniel, Isaiah, Jeremiah and Ezekiel. This section will highlight the relationship between the Book of Revelation and the Old Testament with the aim of discovering how John used his sources and what this means for the task of interpretation. The source-critical approach to Revelation, while not being in any way a new interpretive method, will be presented here due to its relationship to a newer interpretive framework, intertextuality.

## Source-criticism and Revelation's use of the Old Testament

The structural complexity of the book of Revelation, compounded by the presence of repetitions, intercalations, and the lack of smooth narrative development, has led many interpreters to stipulate that John used a number of sources to write his Apocalypse. Source-criticism, a biblical studies method, experienced wide-ranging popularity between the end of the nineteenth and the beginning of the twentieth century. Proponents of this approach were extremely confident in their capacity to identify the presence of various oral or written sources within the biblical books. This is well exemplified by the documentary hypothesis concerning the Pentateuch, the first five books of the Bible. According to this hypothesis, four different documents, or traditions, would have been used by a final redactor to give these five biblical books the shape they have today. Applied to the book of Revelation, this identification of sources has also been prolific. However, there has been very little lasting impact due to a lack of consensus between interpreters.

Three majors types of source-critical theories developed through the years (See Aune, 1998, pp. cx–cxvi for a full presentation). The first type is called *compilation theory*. This hypothesis suggests that two or more apocalypses were combined to form the book of Revelation as we have it today. An example of this was offered by Josephine Massyngberde Ford in her 1975 commentary on Revelation. She stated that chapters 4.1 – 11.19 formed a revelation that had been given to John the Baptist, while 12.1 – 19.21 belonged to one of his disciples. Chapters 1–3 would have been added by a former disciple of John who converted to the Christian faith.

The second type of source-critical theory is called *revision theory*. This approach states that there existed an initial document written by John which would have been expanded or edited by one or more subsequent redactors. One of the most well-known proponents of this theory was the British scholar R. H. Charles who, in his classic commentary on the Apocalypse (1920), stipulated that John the original writer was responsible for having authored 1.1 – 20.3. A not-so-skilled disciple was regarded by Charles as having added 20.4 – 22.21, as well as many other interpolations throughout the main part of the book.

The third kind of source-critical theory is referred to as *fragmentary theory*. Supporters of this approach hold that the writer of Revelation incorporated a number of written sources in his document. Wilhelm Bousset, whose commentary appeared at the start of the twentieth century, proposed that Revelation included five written documents. Among them he identified a Jewish pamphlet made up of 7.1–8 and 11.1–13, as well as a myth found in 12.1–17.

These three types of source-critical theories have faced serious questioning from the majority of interpreters because of their highly subjective nature. Some writers have pushed this approach to the extreme limit, as in the case of Bruce Malina who holds that most of John's Apocalypse was based on ancient astrological and astronomical sources (1995). The recent rise of literary criticism applied to the Bible has strongly emphasized the unity of the biblical documents. Regardless of source identification, literary criticism concentrates on the final product which stands as a unified whole in front of the reader.

It is, however, near impossible to deny that John did use different sources when he wrote down his visions. It is almost self-evident to the majority of interpreters that the Old Testament was John's main source. Any reader who is familiar with the Hebrew Scriptures will rapidly be struck by some of John's images and expressions. It has been calculated that of Revelation's 404 verses, John has included more than 200 allusions to various books of the Old Testament. But there is a catch. John never directly quoted from any of them. This means that he never repeated word for word a full verse of the Old Testament. The fact that everything is allusion instead of quotation has made it difficult to calculate exactly how many of them are present in the book of Revelation. Allusions can go from being *direct*, meaning that the wording and meaning are almost similar, to *probable*, with some vocabulary linked to the original, but with some departure from the meaning, to *possible*, with only a few words corresponding, like an echo.

Another point of discussion in John's use of the Old Testament is whether it took place consciously or not. Any actual quote from a specific passage in the Old Testament would have made it hard to argue that he did this unconsciously, even though it would still be possible. However, since all he did was to allude to passages instead of quoting them, the question of his intention in doing so remains shrouded in controversy. If John's mind, like that of any other Jewish male, had been flooded from his youth with passages from the Holy Scriptures, it could very well be that some of them would come out naturally while he was trying to make a point. Nonetheless, some of the allusions are so clear that it becomes problematic to deny that John actually intended for his readers to reflect on a specific passage of the Old Testament.

The faithfulness of John in regard to the context of the passages he used has also been debated (See Beale, 1999, pp. 81–86, 97–99, and

Moyise, 1995 for related discussions). The term 'context' here includes literary, historical and thematic aspects. Did John pay attention to the role a specific passage played in the book to which it belonged? Did he take into consideration the period of Israel's history in which this passage originated? Or, did he pay more attention to the theme or themes evoked by a specific allusion? This could have influenced the way in which his allusions were to be interpreted.

Some commentators have suggested that John often disregarded the original context of his Old Testament source. They argued that he was addressing Gentile congregations who did not have the scriptural knowledge required to fully interpret his references, and that, as a Christian prophet, he was not interested in interpreting Scriptures (Swete, Thomas, Schüssler Fiorenza). They could add that John, contrary to someone like Matthew, never used expressions like 'this took place to fulfill what had been spoken by the Lord through the prophet' (Matt 1.22). Other interpreters, including Gregory Beale (1999), have challenged these assumptions by pointing to the fact that John's congregations included a large number of Jewish Christians as well as God-fearers, Gentiles who followed the Jewish faith while refusing to be circumcised. Another argument invoked is that John might have intended his hearers to actually go back to the original passage in order to interpret what he was presenting. This will be examined in further detail later on.

By examining some passages from the book of Revelation we are able to highlight the various allusions and echoes of the Old Testament they bring to mind. John's main sources were: the Pentateuch, the Psalms, the minor prophets, as well as the books of Daniel, Ezekiel and Isaiah. The first vision John had of Christ is a good starting point. The passage is the following:

> and in the midst of the lampstands I saw one like the Son of Man, clothed with a long robe and with a golden sash across his chest. His head and his hair were white as white wool, white as snow; his eyes were like a flame of fire, his feet were like burnished bronze, refined as in a furnace, and his voice was like the sound of many waters. In his right hand he held seven stars, and from his mouth came a sharp, two-edged sword, and his face was like the sun shining with full force. (Rev. 1.13–16)

Looking at the cross-reference system of the New Revised Standard Version one sees that the main allusion is to Daniel 10.5–6:

> I looked up and saw a man clothed in linen, with a belt of gold from Uphaz around his waist. His body was like beryl, his face like lightning, his eyes like flaming torches, his arms and legs like the gleam of burnished bronze, and the sound of his words like the roar of a multitude.

To this could be added Daniel 7.13a: 'As I watched in the night visions, I saw one like a son of man coming with the clouds of heaven.' Steve Moyise (1995) has offered an interesting analysis of the various Old Testament allusions found in this passage. In addition to what we have already presented, he has identified further allusions such as: Ezekiel 9.11 'Then the man clothed in linen, with the writing case at his side' and Daniel 7.9 'and an Ancient One took his throne, his clothing was white as snow, and the hair of his head like pure wool ...' (1995, pp. 37–8).

It is interesting to notice that John did not limit himself to only one specific passage in order to paint his picture of Christ, but that he multiplied the references until he reached the nuances and effect desired.

Another striking example of John's use of the Old Testament is his description of the beast in Revelation 13.1–2:

> And I saw a *beast* rising *out of the sea*, having ten horns and seven heads; and on its horns were ten diadems, and on its heads were blasphemous names. And the beast that I saw was like a *leopard*, its feet were like a *bear*'s, and its mouth was like a *lion*'s mouth. And the dragon gave it his power and his throne and great authority.

The main passage referred to is Daniel 7.3–6:

> and four great *beasts* came up *out of the sea*, different from one another. The first was like a *lion* and had eagles' wings. Then, as I watched, its wings were plucked off, and it was lifted up from the ground and made to stand on two feet like a human being; and a human mind was given to it. Another beast appeared, a second one, that looked like a *bear*. It was raised up on one side, had three tusks in its mouth among its teeth and was told, 'Arise, devour many bodies!' After this, as I watched, another appeared, like a *leopard*. The beast had four wings of a bird on its back and four heads; and dominion was given to it.

The ten horns might have alluded to Daniel 7.7, 20, 24:

> After this I saw in the visions by night a fourth beast, terrifying and dreadful and exceedingly strong. It had great iron teeth and was devouring, breaking in pieces, and stamping what was left with its feet. It was different from all the beasts that preceded it, and it had *ten horns* ... and concerning the *ten horns* that were on its head, and concerning the other horn, which came up and to make room for which three of them fell out – the horn that had eyes and a mouth that spoke arrogantly, and that seemed greater than the others ... As for the *ten horns*, out of this kingdom ten kings shall arise, and another shall arise after them. This one shall be different from the former ones, and shall put down three kings.

Once again, John felt free to use the text of the Old Testament in order to make his point. The four beasts of Daniel became one in John. Further down, the ten horns are given a meaning similar to that used by Daniel. This passage in Revelation would have easily brought to mind Daniel's description of the four beasts. Many other passages of Revelation could be listed with the numerous allusions written in a parallel column.

The last stop in this study of John's use of the Old Testament concerns the way in which his hearers were supposed to interpret the allusions. Did John mean for his audience to hearken back to the original passages and use them as a lens through which they could interpret his own message, or did he want them to use his presentation in order to interpret anew the passages of the Old Testament? Intertextuality is an interpretive method which allows a close analysis of this question.

## Intertextuality: unravelling the tapestry of meaning

From the work of Julia Kristeva a concept developed that 'has expanded the ways of accounting for the complex relationship of texts to texts, to interpretive traditions, to writers and readers, and to institutional contexts' (Aichele and Phillips, 1995, p. 7). This approach was named 'intertextuality'. When texts are read by individuals or groups they are brought into interaction with other texts that these same individuals and groups have met before. This encounter situates the work in a web of meaning where the different texts intersect one another. When trying to pinpoint the meaning of John's use of the Old Testament, as well as his respect or disregard for the context(s) of the original passages, we should be mindful of Kristeva's observation that 'in the space of a text several utterances drawn from *other texts intersect and neutralize one another*' (Kristeva, 1969, p. 113). Any written work must be seen as in some way struggling with other texts, called sub-texts, in order to establish its meaning.

This has important consequences for the role of context in John's use of the Old Testament. The meaning comes not solely from the original context of the source nor from the new one into which John embedded this same source, but in the interaction between the two (see Moyise, 1995, ch. 6). When reading a passage in John, one becomes aware of the presence of several allusions to the Old Testament, which in turn, bring along other allusions and contexts. When, in chapter 11, John writes about measuring the temple, the reader is made aware of the reference to Ezekiel 42.15–20. However, the movement does not stop there. The Ezekiel allusion brings with it a series of passages, found throughout the Bible, where the temple is mentioned.

A single allusion used by John represents only a small part of the texture of meaning produced by the interaction between John's text and the Old Testament source he used. This process also requires a high level of involvement on the part of the reader. Every reader comes to the text already possessing an arsenal of texts encountered throughout his or her existence. A specific allusion made by John will provoke a different production of meaning depending on the individual interacting with the text.

This last statement can be illustrated by using John's original audience as an example. Imagine two members of the Pergamum community sitting side by side during a prayer meeting. One of them is Jewish Christian. This means that he/she was raised in a Jewish family and is very familiar with the story of Moses and the exodus. His or her companion is a Gentile who was born and raised somewhere close to Athens. Now, imagine the effect that would be produced on each of these two hearers when the reader proclaimed the chapters relating to the bowls and the plagues.

For the Gentile listener, this passage would merely represent one more punishment sent by God and would be reminiscent of the opening of the seven seals and the blowing of the seven trumpets. On the other hand, the sheer mention of the word plagues, as well as their description, would trigger in the mind of the Jewish listener a series of associations with the story of Moses and the exodus. This in turn would resonate with the coming down to Egypt and the whole situation which had provoked such a move. And the links could go on and on.

This is what intertextuality is all about. Meaning is woven not only by parts of a text interacting with one another, but through the interaction with the sum of all texts which belong to a specific culture as embodied in its various individuals and groups. Intertextuality is a very complex notion. It is much more than mere 'source hunting'. Source-criticism, discussed previously, has had the tendency to see the production of meaning in a very linear way going from the source to the new document in which it is now included. Intertextuality sees the interrelation between source and text as something more interactive.

As John transformed the meaning of his sources by making allusions to them, so was the meaning of his text transformed by them. One could use an image which comes from the study of ancient manuscripts. When looking at an ancient document like the Leningrad codex, which is the oldest complete copy of the Hebrew Scriptures we possess today, one can observe various stains which either block or distort the writing on the page. These stains often made by the ink on the other side of a page are called 'bleedthrough'. It is as if John, when making an allusion, was materially placing his piece of parchment on top of a copy of an

Old Testament passage which was not completely dried yet. The ink from the Old Testament copy would bleed through and affect the characters on John's page, making them harder to read, altering them. This is what happens at the level of meaning every time John alluded to a passage of the Old Testament. Intertextuality, when used in its purest form, deals with transformation of meaning and transformation of reader. This is the challenge it offers to all who wish to enter Revelation's semantic universe.

The newer methods of reading Revelation outlined in this chapter represent only a few of the newer approaches to interpretation. These methods share an emphasis on the effect which the Apocalypse has on contemporary readers. They stress the unity of the text, as well as the participatory role of the reader. We could have included other methods of reading such as deconstruction which was made famous by the French philosopher Jacques Derrida, and applied to Revelation by feminist interpreter Tina Pippin. As well, we could have tackled the complex issue of psychoanalytic interpretation as practised by Julia Kristeva and applied to the Gospels by French psychoanalyst Françoise Dolto. All of these newer approaches have something valuable to contribute to the interpretation of Revelation, even if they rarely find favour within mainstream scholarship. The reader is nevertheless encouraged to explore Revelation from all possible angles in order to discover the manifold truth of John's message.

# 6

## Revelation and Contemporary Christianity

The process of biblical interpretation usually follows a sequence of steps which culminates in the interpreter's attempt to find a specific application for it in the life of the contemporary believer. In the case of the book of Revelation, the question of application has been mostly ignored by mainline Christianity. This is probably due in part to the general disregard accorded this book in the main traditional denominations. The Roman Catholic Church, for example, reads from Revelation only twice in its three-year reading cycle and these passages are secondary to the gospel excerpts accompanying them. The Greek Orthodox church does not read at all from Revelation. Anglican, Methodist and Presbyterian churches also tend to generally follow this pattern. As we have seen in previous chapters, a long history of mistrust has affected the full acceptance and use of the book of Revelation. This in turn has led many to question the relevancy of Revelation for contemporary Christianity.

### Revelation and biblical interpretation

When dealing with the issue of Revelation's relevance for the modern world, one is bound to address a more basic concern which is that of the goal of Bible reading and interpretation. What is it that we try to accomplish when we read the Bible? The answers to this can be varied. Some read the Bible to find spiritual comfort and strength. Others read it because of its literary quality. A third group might read the Bible in the hope of getting a glimpse of life in ancient Israel or the first Christian community. But basically, all approach the text as something which holds meaning for them. But what kind of meaning is to be found in Scriptures? Are all interpretations legitimate?

Since the Bible claims to be the record of an act of communication between God and human authors at definite times in history (Moyise, 1998, pp. 1–12), every reader is faced with the task of trying to understand what this specific communication was all about. However, several obstacles face the interpreter. The first one is that every reader of the Bible occupies the position of third party in the act of communication. Most biblical scholars would agree that each book of the Bible was written for a specific audience living around the time when each of these books was penned. As twenty-first-century believers, we therefore stand outside of this original act of divine/human communication. We must try to identify who the author was, who the original audience was, what the historical circumstances were, as well as a number of other factors. This identification forces one to try and bridge a cultural/historical gap which is constantly present between the contemporary reader and the parties originally involved in the act of communication which resulted in each biblical book. A contemporary reader will never be able to fully understand what the life of a first-century Christian was like. Historical reconstructions are never perfect and are always open to revision. One must therefore be careful not to hold on to them too strongly.

Such an historically minded approach is related to the concept of authorial intent advocated by a large number of biblical interpreters. What is it that the original writer intended to say? What was his purpose in writing this book or letter? While this might seem easy and straightforward, the history of biblical interpretation has proven that the authorial intent is sometimes a fleeting concept. How does one determine the intent of any writer? Can any written communication be a perfectly faithful vehicle and mirror of one's intention and purpose? If yes, why are misunderstandings and misinterpretations such a part of daily human experience, i.e., 'Oh, I thought you meant ...'?

However one deals with the question of authorial intent, all Christians agree that the Bible is the living Word of the Living God, not just some artifact put here for the delight of antiquarians. Therefore, it must be relevant for today's believers. This is where the concept of application comes into play. How can one take instructions presented by Paul in his letters and apply them to the life of the contemporary Christian community? Is it possible to do this with all the books and passages of the Bible or only with a specific number of them? Did the biblical writers put down concepts which they willed to be considered normative for the future Christian community? These are some of the questions facing anyone who wishes to apply the Bible to a modern context in a way which is at once relevant to the contemporary circumstances and respectful of the origin and nature of the biblical books.

Most Christians would agree that a blanket application of the Bible to modern life is impossible. Too many of the situations and regulations found in the Bible are bound to their original context. A process must be undertaken to decide which passages can be transferable to the contemporary situation and to what extent this transfer can take place. It is there that the message of Scriptures will intersect with the needs of the contemporary believing community. This is the task facing anyone trying to make the book of Revelation relevant for today.

## Is Revelation relevant?

Should modern-day Christianity use the book of Revelation at the same rate and with the same eagerness as the Gospels or Paul's main letters? The answer to this question is very much linked to what we have just explored concerning the nature and task of biblical interpretation. Since Revelation is part of the Christian canon, it means that ultimately it was considered by the believing community as representative of God's Word to humanity, at the same level as the Gospels and the Pauline epistles. The resulting correlative is that Revelation, like all other biblical books, contains elements which are applicable to today's situation.

However, most Christian churches have, for various reasons, shied away from using Revelation as a source of encouragement and nourishment for the Christian faithful. Charles Talbert has pointed to three major deterrents to the use of Revelation among the mainline denominations: 1) The apparent inaccessibility of Revelation's meaning, 2) the almost complete absence of pastoral relevance, and 3) Revelation's susceptibility to abuse (1994, pp. 2, 111). Each of these potential obstacles needs to be addressed in order to dispel the uneasiness which affects most Christians when they hear the name Revelation.

### Revelation's inaccessible language

The main obstacle to reading Revelation is its author's use of a highly symbolic form of language. We have already discussed the nature of symbols and how they can be interpreted. However, since many of Revelation's symbols were native to the first-century context, the readers find themselves facing the historical/cultural gap discussed previously. Nevertheless, one should not be afraid to tackle this task. All the books of the Bible contain symbolism to a certain extent. This has never stopped the Church from using these same books in its liturgical and pastoral life; and individual believers from using them in their spiritual life. Any symbol, as we have seen before, is opened to a variety of interpretations, some more accurate than others. Therefore, the symbolic nature of many of Revelation's statements could become a point of entry in applying the message of Revelation to a contemporary setting.

## Revelation and pastoral care

What is the pastoral relevance of the book of Revelation? Can the Christian community use its teachings when dealing with the contemporary world in which it is embedded? One way of answering this question would be to try and identify situations which were present in Revelation's original context and see if such phenomena are still present in today's society in one form or another. This could allow one to transfer Revelation's original message in order to address some contemporary predicaments.

With this kind of methodology in mind, it is possible, according to most scholars, to identify two main situations which might have supplied John with his primary impetus to write Revelation: 1) Christians going through difficult times facing either socio-economic ostracism, public pressure, or persecution, and wondering if it is worth it to still believe in God's rule over humanity's destiny, and 2) the temptation faced by some believers to compromise their faith in favour of complete acceptance from their pagan neighbours. Many scholars hold to one of these two while excluding the other. This kind of either/or attitude is not warranted in this case since both states of affairs could have been simultaneously affecting a given congregation or one could have affected a given community while the other affected a different group. It would be considerably more profitable to consider both as valid. Consequently, if this assessment is correct, John's answer to such happenings might become relevant to today's believers stuck in similar predicaments or involved in similar behaviours.

Christians, all over the world, still face situations which threaten their very existence as a distinct religious movement. Believers in India, Latin America, Iraq, China and other countries face great danger simply due to the fact that they confess their faith in Christ in the face of intolerant governments and communities. In addition, Christian missionaries are still today being martyred. In the face of such situations, Revelation's message can become a powerful tool to comfort and strengthen the individuals facing such peril. John was consistent in affirming that the ultimate victory belongs to the followers of the Lamb who choose openly to confess their faith in God and His Christ. The image of the 144,000 saved martyrs can be applied to all believers who remain faithful, even unto death.

For Christians who live in quieter environments, like most European countries and those on the North American continent, the challenge and danger they encounter is of a different nature altogether. Instead of facing the threat of imprisonment and death, they end up being constantly challenged by societies which are not based on, and do not advocate, Christian values and principles. The danger such a situation represents is comparable to the AIDS virus; slowly invading the body and gradually taking over the cells which normally detect the presence of a dangerous foreign body and ultimately destroying the whole immune system, thus leaving the individual defenceless. Christians living in highly developed areas are repeatedly bombarded with messages, through music, movies and advertisements, which contradict and undermine the tenets of their faith and the behaviours derived from them. The repetitive nature of such messages produces in many a form of desensitization. After a while, the dissonance disappears and the individuals adopt the values propounded by such advertisements. All this is done at the expense of their Christian faith. This danger of assimilation is even greater for Christians whose faith is weak and whose spiritual life tends to be anaemic. Their spiritual house is built on sand and the wind of any anti-Christian culture will quickly blow it down.

For all who are facing such a situation, Revelation could be used to offer both warning and encouragement. John of Patmos was quick in pointing out the danger faced by believers living in a non-Christian environment which tries to undermine their faith by flooding them with messages that contradict it. In John's original context, the second beast of Revelation 13 seemed to have represented the Roman empire's propaganda machine which relentlessly tried to get everyone to serve the empire and blindly worship its leader. The image of this beast could be legitimately transposed to modern society where consumerism is the second beast serving the first monster: capitalism. Greed is good and money makes the world go round. The number of Christians who have adopted an ethos which is fundamentally contradictory to Gospel values is astonishing. They can participate in Sunday service, sharing communion with their fellow congregants, and the next morning fire two hundred employees without any regard to the devastating effects this will have on these individuals' lives and that of their respective families.

John was clear in stating that Christians cannot assimilate, nor can they compromise in any way with an alien ethos which endangers their Christian distinctiveness. In Revelation, all followers of the beast ended up in the lake of fire. The message to the church of Laodicea went straight to the point: 'I know your works; you are neither cold nor hot. I wish that you were either cold or hot. So, because you are lukewarm, and neither cold nor hot, I am about to spit you out of my mouth' (Rev 3.15–16). Compromise, in John's opinion, spelt idolatry. Contemporary Christianity seems to be in dire need of this kind of warning. Charles Talbert pointed out that Revelation

> speaks a word of warning to the unthinking mass of Christians who simply want to share in the economic fruits of Babylon's wealth and luxury and are quite willing to assimilate in order to reap the temporal benefits ... those with upward social mobility who want to be totally immersed in the larger society and are consciously willing to lose their souls in order to do so. (1994, p. 112)

This danger becomes even greater when the proponents of assimilation and compromise are leaders of the church. John was conscious of this and did not recoil from attacking supporters of such a compromise, e.g., Jezebel and the Nicolaitans. A Christianity which aims at being comfortable with the surrounding culture, instead of working at transforming it, is already on the path to full assimilation.

## Revelation's susceptibility to abuse

Mainline Christianity's fear and discomfort with the book of Revelation has left the door open for its use and abuse by fringe groups and doomsday cults. Its seeming lack of relevance, which we have just refuted above, has encouraged its being disregarded by the majority of churches. Some examples of marginal conventicles which have misused Revelation were given in the introduction to this book. This abuse will continue to manifest itself until all main Christian groups reclaim and regain the book of Revelation as integral part of their Holy Scriptures. If the book of Revelation is marginalized, it will keep on attracting marginal individuals and groups. Christian denominations must take a stand on acceptable interpretations of the book. Lines must be drawn concerning the way in which symbols function and can be interpreted. Churches and their pastors must overcome their discomfort with Revelation, and their lack of knowledge, and actively start expounding the book's message to their congregants. Only an informed Christian will be able to critique the number of worthless, fear-mongering, books being constantly published on Revelation.

Scholars who specialize in the study of Revelation will have to make their work available to the general readership if they want to see their theological discoveries influence the way in which Revelation is used. This includes more than publishing for their peers and resting content with the academia's seal of approval. The majority of the population must be exposed to the extensive conclusions drawn by exegetes on its own terms. Failure to communicate effectively such discoveries to the masses will only result in popular, end-of-the-world, apocalyptic books outselling legitimate commentaries.

## Revelation's theology

In the quest to make Revelation relevant for modern society, another alternative seems to present itself. This option consists in focusing on the general message which the book offers concerning God, Christ and the Holy Spirit, in other words, its theology. Revelation's theological message possesses the capacity to remain relevant notwithstanding particular interpretations of the book as prophecy, apocalypse or letter. It would be good for the contemporary Christian community to focus on this specific aspect of the book, which very often is disregarded in favour of detailed study of the trumpets, plagues, and bowls, the number of the beast, the thousand-year reign, etc. Certain elements, which could be considered foundational to any attempt at reconstructing the theology of Revelation, need to be examined.

Through the years, many Christian theologians have been very uneasy with the images of God and Christ found within the book of Revelation. The figure of Christ depicted through the Apocalypse seems, at first sight, to contradict the portrait painted by Gospel passages such as the Sermon on the Mount. How can a Christ who entreated his followers to love their enemies and turn the other cheek be reconciled with the warrior figure of the Apocalypse who wreaks destruction upon large segments of humanity? Is the Christ of Revelation and his God reconcilable with the traditional Christian faith? A superficial reading of Revelation might lead one to answer this last question in the negative. However, a detailed study of the theology and Christology of the Apocalypse seems to favour an affirmative answer.

### The God of Revelation

The book of Revelation is one of the most theocentric books in the whole Bible. John's presentation of God's being and his ultimate sovereignty over the universe is among the most impressive. Divine self-revelations punctuate the text at its beginning and its end. In Revelation 1.8 God defines himself in the following terms: 'I am the Alpha and the Omega, says the Lord God, who is and who was and who is to come, the Almighty.' The letter alpha is the first letter of the Greek alphabet and omega the last one. Thus God is presented as being the first and the last. Incidentally, this designation of first and last will appear later on in the book as a title for Christ. This identification of

God as first and last is reinforced by the second divine self-designation found at 21.6: 'I am the Alpha and the Omega, the beginning and the end.' This appellation of God as first and last, is linked to passages in the book of Isaiah. In Isaiah 44.6 God says: 'I am the first and I am the last, besides me there is no god.' At 48.12 He reiterates: 'I am He; I am the first, and I am the last.' As Richard Bauckham so aptly pointed out, 'the designation encapsulates the understanding of the God of Israel as the sole Creator of all things and sovereign Lord of History ... God precedes all things, as their Creator, and he will bring all things to eschatological fulfillment. He is the origin and goal of all history' (1993, p. 27).

Nothing truly exists but him. The God of Genesis 1, who uttered 'Let there be light' to bring creation into being, is the same one who concludes 'It is done' when the new creation has been fulfilled. Nothing can escape the presence of God. This is one of two reasons why faithful believers can already rejoice in their ultimate victory while undergoing persecution. They know that everything is in the hands of the One in whom they have put their faith.

The next powerful image representative of God, in Revelation, is that of the One sitting on the throne. This expression was used numerous times to represent God. God's throne was located in heaven and represented once again his ultimate sovereignty over all that exists. Such a representation of God was linked to prophetic visions as found in Isaiah 6.1–3:

> In the year that King Uzziah died, I saw the Lord sitting on a throne, high and lofty; and the hem of his robe filled the temple. Seraphs were in attendance above him; each had six wings: with two they covered their faces, and with two they covered their feet, and with two they flew. And one called to another and said: 'Holy, holy, holy is the LORD of hosts; the whole earth is full of his glory.'

and Ezekiel 1.26:

> And above the dome over their heads there was something like a throne, in appearance like sapphire; and seated above the likeness of a throne was something that seemed like a human form.

John's theology was thus strongly imbedded in Jewish monotheism and maybe also in a form of spirituality known as Merkabah mysticism, where the participant would try to reach the highest level of contemplation and gaze upon God's throne (Hebrew: *merkabah*, meaning chariot). This heavenly point of view allows the visionary John to correctly interpret the visions he receives concerning events taking place on earth and affirm that those who seem to be losing the battle on earth are in fact reaping victory in heaven.

This God is the only one worthy of being worshipped. Often times, the expression 'the One who sits on the throne' is accompanied by a description of heavenly worship. The four creatures, the twenty-four elders, all heavenly creatures, and everything that exists on earth and underneath the earth worships this ultimate Sovereign. This powerful description of universal worship confirms God's being as Eternal ruler, Almighty and Creator.

## The Christ of Revelation

Jean-Pierre Prévost, in his 1983 book on Revelation (*Pour en Finir avec la Peur*), asked the following question: 'Is Revelation a book about the end of the world or about Christ?' (1983, p. 11, my translation). He then, further on, answered this question by emphasizing the centrality of Christ in Revelation. This is one aspect of the book which often eludes the general readership. The occasional reader of Revelation tends to be engrossed by the figures of the four horsemen, the calamities provoked by the opening of the seals, the blowing of the trumpets, and the pouring of the bowls, and consequently forgets to pay attention to what the book is affirming concerning Christ.

In chapter 2 it was presented that the character of Christ is central to the narrative aspect of the book of Revelation. Among his many aliases we identified those of the One like the Son of Man (1.13; 14.14), the slain/yet standing Lamb (6.6; 14.1), the male child (12.5), and the rider on the white horse (19.11). However, Revelation offers much more than just various appellations for Christ. The book is a repository of information concerning Christ's role in God's redemptive history as well as his sharing in God's divinity and sovereignty. Some of the titles bestowed on Christ in the Apocalypse are original to this book, e.g., The Alpha and the Omega, the slain Lamb, the Prince of life, the Lion of Judah, etc. Prévost highlighted four main Christological themes in the book of Revelation: Christ as slain Lamb, Christ as the Living, Christ as the Lord, and Christ as principle of the new creation. (1983, pp. 16–17). Let us examine the first two.

The title of 'Lamb' in Revelation appears 29 times, using the Greek word *arnion* instead of *amnos* as found in the Gospel of John. This designation encompasses all of the Paschal mystery. Christ is the Lamb whose blood has led the new Israel through its own exodus. His blood gave eternal life to all who believe in him. Though slain he is still alive, standing on the throne of God, reigning with him, and with him receiving honour and glory from all of creation (Rev. 5.9–14).

The title of Christ as the Living is closely associated to the Lamb terminology. Through his resurrection, Christ has become the ultimate example of life. This new life which he has gained through his death is the life which he will impart to his followers whose names are written in the book of life. As Prévost concluded: 'The Christ of Revelation is the living *par excellence* and it is the conviction of Christians that only he can give Life' (1983, p. 16, italics and translation mine).

The Christology of Revelation is one of the most original in all of the New Testament writings. John's theology constantly hammered home the point that God and Christ are one, and that both are the only ones worthy of glory, honour and worship. Bauckham justly high-lighted John's desire to affirm Christ's divinity. This can be seen in the use John made of parallel, synonymous expressions for Christ and God.

> God: I am the Alpha and the Omega. (1.9)
> Christ: I am the first and the last. (1.17)
> God: I am the Alpha and the Omega, the beginning and the end. (21.6)
> Christ: I am the Alpha and the Omega, the first and the last, the beginning and the end (22.13). (Bauckham 1993, pp. 54–55)

This unity between God and Christ makes him worthy to exercise universal sovereignty and dominion at the same level as God. This makes John's Christology one of the most powerful expositions of Christ's being and of his role in God's redemptive history.

## The Spirit in Revelation

In order to conclude our brief study of the theology found within the book of Revelation, it is only fitting to address the question of the third person of the Trinity, the Holy Spirit. Is he represented in the Apocalypse, and if so, how? What function(s) does he exercise in Revelation? The term 'spirit' or 'spirits' as relating to the Spirit of God, is found eighteen times in the book of Revelation. These occurrences can be subdivided in three main categories: a) the word 'spirit' used within the expression 'in the spirit', b) ten general references to the Spirit, and c) four mentions of the seven spirits of God.

a) The expression 'in the spirit' occurs four times in Revelation (1.10; 4.2; 17.3; 21.10). In chapter one, the visionary experience of John was discussed in relation to this expression. When John used such language, he seemed to be pointing to the ecstatic, or trance-like state he experienced when receiving the visions. The Spirit became the agent of these experiences. The last three instances listed above seem to connote an experience within the ecstatic state where John finds himself being transported to heaven and to the wilderness. The word 'spirit' in these four passages represents the Spirit of God as agent of the visionary experience, and does not refer to any body/spirit dichotomy.

b) The word 'spirit' occurs ten times within a more general context. Within this group, seven mentions of the spirit are found at the end of each letter to the seven churches: 'Let anyone who has an ear listen to what the Spirit is saying to the churches' (Rev 2.7, 11, 17, 29; 3.6, 13, 22). These passages emphasize the divine provenance of the admonitions found within the letters. Two more occurrences quote what the Spirit says (14.13; 22.17), while a last mention of the Spirit is found in the phrase 'the Spirit of prophecy' (19.10). The Spirit, especially in the seven letters, seem to be closely associated to the prophetic mandate of John.

c) The last group of passages mentioning the word 'spirit' is composed of four references to the 'seven spirits of God' (1.4; 3.1; 4.5; 5.6). Of all the uses of the word 'spirit' in the book of Revelation, this is the one which has fed the greatest amount of discussion between interpreters. The two basic interpretations which have been offered are the following:

1. Seven spirits as representing the fullness of the Holy Spirit (Bauckham, Beale, Wall, Caird, Johnson). Seven being the symbol for fullness and completeness, the seven spirits are said to represent the fullest expression of the presence of the Holy Spirit in the world. John would have come up with this representation of the Spirit through his exegesis of Zechariah 4.1–10. The Spirit is God's and the Lamb's agent in the world. He is the one addressing the churches as witnessed by the expression, 'Let anyone who has an ear listen to what the Spirit is saying to the churches', seen above.

2. Seven spirits as the seven archangels of Jewish theology who are said to stand in the presence of God (Charles, Aune, Massyngberde Ford, Thompson, Roloff). These authors maintain that the interpretation of the seven spirits in Revelation should not be burdened by later Trinitarian dogmas. Even if the word 'spirit' is rarely used in the Old Testament to refer to angels, they frequently point to examples of such usage as found in Qumranian literature. The seven spirits are thus said to represent the seven archangels: Uriel, Raphael, Raguel, Michael, Saraqael, Remiel and Gabriel. Gerhard Krodel seems to have wanted to save both interpretations by stating that: 'The Holy Spirit is pictured here as seven spirit-angels who stand before God's throne' (1989, p. 83), while Mounce suggested that they might represent part of God's heavenly entourage (1998, p. 48).

Any discussion of the relevance of Revelation for contemporary Christianity should centre on the theology found in the book. Readers must get past the strange imagery, and sometimes morbid obsession with trying to predict the future, and use the book's theology to live their lives as faithful Christians facing a brand new millennium. Interpretations of the symbols often refer either to the past or to the future. The theology of Revelation, however, can speak to Christians today, in the here and now.

## A multi-pronged approach to Revelation

In order effectively to use Revelation in a contemporary setting, the Church needs to resolve a debate which has been picking up momentum for the past thirty years, within the world of biblical interpretation. This controversy deals with the use of diachronic methods versus synchronic ones. In the preceding chapter, we have already touched upon the basic difference between these two approaches. If we were to illustrate the process of interpretation using the image of two lines intersecting at a 90° angle, the diachronic methods would be represented by the vertical axis and the synchronic methods by the horizontal one. What this model practically represents for the interpretation of any document can be summarized in the following way.

A diachronic method looks at the historical background of the book, trying to pinpoint its origin as well as the different factors which influenced its coming to existence. Social, economic, political and personal factors are considered to be decisive in the interpretation of the document. The goal is to concentrate solely on the meaning the work had for its original readers and the meaning which the author meant to convey. This has been the traditional way in which biblical studies have functioned.

A synchronic method, on the other hand, concentrates on the status of the written work as it stands today, when read by a contemporary individual. This type of method allows the reader to use the work in any way which can fulfil his or her needs and aspirations. The conditions which gave rise to the book and the author's intention remain in the background but are considered to be irrelevant to the reader's encounter with the text.

The past fifteen years have seen the value of the diachronic critical methods of interpretation come under thorough criticism. The weakness of most of these methods, taken in isolation, is that the biblical text often ends up being looked at through a reductionist approach, a dismembering lens that produces only sterile practical results for one's life of faith. A preterist approach to Revelation is a striking example of this. All that is emphasized is related to the past with almost no links made to the contemporary situation of the reader.

The great advantage of the synchronic approach to interpretation is that it concentrates mostly on the individual's needs and personal situation. The Word of God is allowed to present and act out its multifaceted nature. The reader feels encouraged, exhorted, comforted, strengthened, etc. It ultimately shows that the power of the Word resides in the fact that it is the Word of the *Living* God. This, in the case of Revelation, is well illustrated by the narrative and liberation approaches. When read within the story framework, Revelation becomes a drama into which the readers can project themselves. When read from the perspective of the poor and oppressed of South and Latin America, it becomes a stinging critique of Western capitalism.

Paul R. Noble tried to answer the question of the relevance of each set of methods and the relationship that might exist between them. While noting that 'critical and literary [synchronic] interpretations typically yield quite different *kinds* of understanding' (1993, p. 131), he emphasized that the two families of methods need each other in order to minimize the possibility of misinterpretation. The two approaches must be considered complementary in order to mine fully the richness of the text at hand:

> The text was produced in a particular historical-critical situation, knowledge of which is indispensable for a sensitive synchronic reading; and conversely, historical reconstructions of what lies behind a text are dependent upon an accurate literary appreciation of the text's final form. (Noble, 1993, p. 131)

Allen Dwight Callahan's analysis of the language of the Apocalypse stressed that the synchronic methods seem to be called for simply by the way in which the original audience received Revelation's message. He emphasized that: 'those first ancient auditors of the Apocalypse came together ... to undergo a collective change in consciousness ... the reading of the Apocalypse moved its hearers, affected them; the text *did* something to them' (1995, p. 460). Because, as Callahan presented, this language was consciously used by the author of Revelation, as an 'idiolectical' tool, the role of the hearer/reader became central. Such an analysis legitimizes the use of synchronic methods such as feminist criticism in the interpretation of Revelation.

The main question in this debate could be stated as this: What is the role of the readers? Is it to go in search of a certain meaning already present in the text, like some kind of buried treasure, or is it to project themselves into the text and take out of it what is relevant to their personal situation? Proponents of the diachronic methods would lean toward the first option, while the second part of the question would be favoured by supporters of the synchronic methods. Revelation's capacity to talk to the contemporary believer hinges on the answer churches will offer to the preceding interrogation. This author believes that interpreters will have to break down their interpretive walls and accept to recognize the good which exists in competing interpretations. The dry little bits of meaning characteristic of the atomistic tendency of the diachronic methods will have to be supplemented by the dynamic, personal aspect of most synchronic interpretations.

The debate concerning Revelation's genre, apocalypse, prophecy or letter, will have to move toward an acceptance of the importance of all three within the interpretive process. If John included these genres within his composition, it was probably for a good reason. Any interpreter who discards one genre automatically impoverishes his or her interpretation of the book. The same is to be said of the traditional approaches to Revelation. Idealists will have to consider preterist and futurist interpretations, and vice versa. The book of Revelation is so complex as to defy any narrow, single-minded approach to it. It is the nature of the beast (no pun intended). The failure of any interpretation to become consensus has thoroughly proven that Revelation has yet to yield more meaning than what has already been unearthed.

Ultimately, interpretation, taking ownership of a text, is an act of re-creation; similar to a Mozart concerto being in some way re-created as it is interpreted by the various musicians who perform it. However, we should not jump to the conclusion that every interpretation is the sole result of communal or individual subjectivity. Interpretation of any concerto would not exist if the concerto was not already open to this possibility. The concerto remains the condition of its interpretation. The book of Revelation could not be interpreted and actualized if it were not already in itself the condition and possibility of all interpretations. Because of its status as historical and living, this parcel of God's Word begs to be interpreted and actualized.

The apocalyptic fever surrounding the new millennium and the danger of sectarian interpretations of the Book of Revelation urge us to find a more holistic way to interpret it. As biblical interpretation experiences a certain paradigm shift, this new way must be one which will avoid the 'dry' results yielded by the historical-critical, diachronic methods and the 'everything goes' mood often present in the synchronic methods.

## Revelation for yesterday, today, and tomorrow

It is ironic to realize that the blessing found in Revelation 1.3 'Blessed is the one who reads aloud the words of the prophecy' has more than once become a curse for the whole Christian community. Among the books of the Bible, none has experienced a more tortuous history of interpretation and application than the book of Revelation. From the early Christian community facing heretical use of the book, to the interpretive abuses manifested in the 1990s by various cults, the book of Revelation has gained an aura of mystery and awe comparable to no other biblical work. We have already seen that its subject matter, its genres, and its omnipresent use of symbols are in part responsible for this state of affairs. The resurgence of its use at critical moments in Western history is quite remarkable.

The first three centuries of Christianity saw the book of Revelation rise to the status of normative Christian writing. However, even though its acceptance was geographically widespread, many influential figures in the Church viewed it suspiciously, among them the great Jerome, translator of the Vulgate, the first authoritative Latin translation of Scriptures. The ease with which it could be interpreted in support of heretical teachings convinced many that the best way to use Revelation was not to use it at all. Before the Middle Ages were ushered in, an implied condition came to be attached to the interpretation of Revelation. This condition was that only an allegorical, moralizing approach could be used to interpret it. Any literal interpretation would likely bring condemnation on the poor soul attempting such a feat.

During the Middle Ages, the birth of the mendicant orders (Franciscans, Dominicans) and the rise of various heretical groups (Beguins, Fraticelli, Lollards) throughout Europe revived the use of the book of Revelation and once again fed the debate as to its nature and usefulness. Not since the time of the Montanist heresy had Revelation become the central theological weapon of so many groups and individuals in their fight against the established Church. Two elements found in the Apocalypse of John ended up monopolizing the debate: the question of the millennium and the identity of the Antichrist.

The greatest interpreter of Revelation during the Middle Ages was a Cistercian monk by the name of Joachim of Fiore (c. 1135–1202). Joachim was an apocalyptically minded preacher who declared himself the recipient of a new prophecy. He sought to reform society and Church as a whole and functioned as an advisor to both popes and civil rulers. The Calabrian monk wrote the first complete historicist interpretation of the Apocalypse. He maintained that the symbols found in the book of Revelation were linked to historical events which had already taken place and gave veiled information as to what would happen in the future. Joachim saw Revelation as a document unveiling the whole historical process, past, present and future. He divided world history in three periods, the last one being the Age of the Spirit, a thousand year period which would follow the Antichrist's defeat. Toward the end of the Middle Ages, Revelation had gained an unprecedented status among the Christian canon, sometimes equalling and even surpassing the Gospels themselves.

All through the troubled years known as the Reformation, the book of Revelation once again surfaced as a theological/political weapon. This time around it was used in the fight between the national churches and the Roman papacy. The question of the identification of the Antichrist took centre stage for Luther and most churches of the Reformation. But even if the Protestants needed to label the pope as Antichrist, the different interpretations offered by the Reformers did vary. One Reformer, Heinrich Bullinger, moved away from the literal interpretation of the Reformation churches and fell back on an approach based on moralism and allegory. John Calvin, the great Genevan reformer, never commented nor preached on the Revelation of John. This was an exceptional situation since Calvin wrote commentaries on all the other books of the New Testament. Even more, the Reformed church decided, in 1596, that no one could comment or preach on Revelation without the express permission of the provincial synod. Ulrich Zwingli, the Swiss reformer, was very suspicious of Revelation, especially of its angelology (theory about angels). In his opinion, Revelation was an incentive to a kind of sterile pious mysticism among the Christian masses.

The Age of Reason gave rise to the historical-critical method of interpretation, which did much to defuse the ominous aura of the book of Revelation. In an age where the scientific method was the measuring rod for everything under the sun, literal interpretations of Revelation's symbolism were bound to raise eyebrows. Even so, theories intent on predicting the future by using Revelation's symbols remained popular with a segment of interpreters known as 'dispensationalists'.

The last two centuries have been marked by opposite approaches to the book of Revelation, that of biblical studies, namely the historical-critical methods, and popular interpretations offered by various sectarian and cultic groups. The movement known as the Millerites remains the ultimate example of the latter. William Miller (1782–1849) was a retired army officer who became a Baptist lay preacher. His study of the Bible concentrated mostly on the books of Daniel and Revelation. Through a series of calculations, supported with graphs and charts, Miller came to the conclusion that the end would take place sometime in 1843. This, obviously, did not happen.

However, the Millerite movement did not die, it merely reincarnated itself in movements like the Seventh-Day Adventist church, the Jehovah's Witnesses, and the Branch Davidians. The leaders of these various groups tried again and again to predict the end of the world by using the book of Revelation as a guide. History, however, has stifled them every time. Despite all of this, the doomsday mentality is still very much present. The well-known American televangelist Jerry Falwell, on 2 February 1999, predicted the coming of the Antichrist in the next ten years, triggering the rapture. Many people seem to ignore the lessons of history and are willing to repeat its worst mistakes.

The book of Revelation awaits a new epoch in the history of its interpretation. After the apocalyptic frenzy has subsided and doomsday gurus are done trying to find reasons why the end of the world did not happen, Revelation's message will still be there, ready to be heard anew. It is hoped that the mainstream Christian churches will take this opportunity to make peace with a document they have mistreated, abused and too often ignored.

# 7

## Studying Revelation

As a written testament to the faith of one early Christian visionary, the book of Revelation offers its readers a variety of viewpoints from which it can be enjoyed and studied. The preceding chapters have offered ways in which the book is read and interpreted today. But how does one undertake to study the book of Revelation? Where does one start? This chapter will strive to offer the reader various paths which might lead one to encounter Revelation at a more personal level, whether spiritual or academic.

### Reading and studying Revelation as individual and church

The book of Revelation has fascinated believers and non-believers alike throughout the centuries. A variety of people have used it for widely different reasons. This remains the greatest witness to the power of this book. Whether to fulfil spiritual or intellectual needs, individuals have searched Revelation looking for answers to questions regarding their faith, their present experience, and sometimes their future. But, how is a fruitful study of Revelation performed? In what context, personal or communal? From a scholarly perspective, a spiritual one, or both?

When enjoying any book of the Bible, Christians tend to follow modern reading habits which usually consist in sitting somewhere by oneself and silently going through the book. The first pointer to anyone wanting to study Revelation, or the Gospels or Paul's letters for that matter, in an individual way, would be to revert to the way ancients used to read any text. In antiquity, reading was always done aloud. Even when sitting alone in a room, people would read the book in the same way it would be read in front of a group, that is out loud. An example of this is found in Acts 8.30, where Philip runs to the chariot of the Ethiopian eunuch and hears him reading the book of the prophet Isaiah. Another example is found in the writings of St Augustine who, when talking of his relationship with St Ambrose, tells how surprised he was when he realized that Ambrose would often read by himself, *in silence*.

The fact of reading aloud allows the use of a greater number of senses. In the case of Revelation, this becomes a tremendous way of enhancing one's reading experience, especially since it is such a sensory book. Words tend to impress themselves deeper in the reader's mind when read aloud. Such a way of reading forces the individual to pay attention to all the words present on the page instead of, quite unconsciously, skipping over some of them. This also brings the contemporary reader one step closer to the experience of Revelation's first recipients. As well, it could be a way to partake of the beatitude found at 1.3a 'Blessed is the one who reads aloud the words of the prophecy …' However, this beatitude, viewed in its original context, took the reading experience one step further.

The literacy level in ancient society tended to be quite low. Individuals were taught to read at a minimum level, one that would enable most people to deal with basic forms of writing: personal letters, lists, simple contracts. Very few people, comparatively speaking, would read full literary works or even have access to them. The absence of mechanical copying devices made scrolls and codices (books) an extremely rare and valuable possession. In the case of letters being sent from one individual to a group of people, the missive would usually be read aloud to the group. This latter behaviour is the one directly addressed by the above-mentioned beatitude. The reading of Revelation, in the first Christian communities, was done out loud. One member of the congregation, probably the one with the best reading skills, would read the book out to the rest of the congregation. The experience, for the majority of believers, would therefore be completely aural in nature, involving intense listening and concentration on the reading being done. The disadvantage of such a procedure would be that, in case of doubt as to what had just been read, the *lector* would probably not interrupt his/her reading to go back a few verses. What would have been the best context for such a communal experience of the book of Revelation?

The presence of various hymns throughout Revelation has led the majority of interpreters to suggest that the public reading of this book was done within a liturgical setting, mostly that of the Sunday gathering used to commemorate the resurrection of Christ. It is within this context that the message and experience offered by the Apocalypse of John would reach its maximum effect. Within this liturgical setting, the hearers' minds were ready to get in touch with the world of the divine, the world of angels and living creatures. Liturgy created sacred time, a time when the common, daily, profane time of existence came to intersect with

God's time and God's world, with the sacred in all its awe and life-transforming power. The hearers would therefore be ready to accompany John in his otherworldly journey. The hymns proclaimed by the four living creatures and the twenty-four elders in Revelation would at that moment become those of the community. Through repeated readings of the book of Revelation, the congregation might also have memorized these hymns and might have used them as an antiphonal prayer during the reading of the book, joining the chorus of the twenty-four elders, the four living creatures and the rest of the heavenly inhabitants. At that moment, earth and heaven, the whole of the material and spiritual universe would join in one unbroken praise to its Lord and God.

This question of the liturgical setting of Revelation has momentous repercussions for the way one should read and study the book. As a second helpful hint in experiencing the book of Revelation, the following is recommended. First of all, the reader should try, at least once, to experience the reading of the book during a liturgical event, accompanied by the Eucharist, or Lord's Supper, or any other form of memorial found in one's own Christian denomination. This would involved getting organized with other believers in order to set up such an event, and getting help from one's priest, minister or pastor to officiate the eucharistic part, if needs be according to each denomination's rules. If organizing a full-blown liturgical event becomes much of an impossibility, believers should try to gather in small prayer groups and experience the reading of the book within such a setting. Preferably, the whole book should be read in one sitting, or if constrained by time and other commitments, divided in two parts, e.g., 1–11, 12–22. Some of the elements of the book could be emphasized by the use of props, like the burning of incense, or actions, like kneeling for some of the hymnic passages. Other elements of the book could be enacted in some limited way. For example, Revelation 8.1 reads: 'When the Lamb opened the seventh seal, there was silence in heaven for about half an hour.' At this point, the reader should pause for a minute or two and allow the congregants to reflect and meditate on what has been read, up to that point. The reading of the book could become an extremely moving and illuminating experience for the participants.

Since the mainline churches make very scarce use of Revelation, it is the responsibility of individual congregational leaders and members to bring the book back into the spiritual, ethical, and scriptural life of their respective community. These two suggestions to reading the book, aloud by oneself or within a liturgical setting, could help many get a better comprehension of the kind of encounter the first Christian communities had with Revelation. This, in turn, could move the individual or group to a more systematic, intellectual study of the text.

# Helps in studying Revelation:
## Commentaries and specialized works

After having experienced the book of Revelation at a liturgical, spiritual level, one might decide to undertake a full-blown exegetical study. While being one of the best ways to uncover the meaning of the book, this task can quickly turn into a mind-boggling experience, especially when trying to identify the starting point of such a study. The amount of literature which exists on the book of Revelation is enough to discourage even the most motivated Bible students. There is a way, however, to ease oneself into a scientific, critical study of Revelation. This mostly consists in acquiring references relevant to one's level of experience in biblical studies and which provide the knowledge needed to allow the reader to subsequently go on to more complex works.

This section endeavours to present some commentaries and other works that could become very useful when studying Revelation. The works are classified first in one of two categories: 1) commentaries and 2) specialized monographs. The commentaries will be classified as introductory, intermediate or advanced. This classification is relative and sometimes difficult to ascertain since some works fall in between two categories. Comments are added to highlight some of the strong points or weaknesses of each work.

## Commentaries

Apart from the biblical text itself, commentaries are the basic tools used in studying any book of the Bible. These usually provide basic information as to the genre, historical background, and main features of the book they address. An explanation of each unit of text follows, becoming more and more detailed depending on the level of the commentary. The following are some well-known works on Revelation, classified *chronologically* within categories based on their individual level of difficulty.

### Introductory
Ladd, George Eldon (1972), *A Commentary on the Revelation of John* (Grand Rapids, Michigan: Eerdmans).

This work is a well laid out, easy to use, exegesis of Revelation. Introductory matters such as authorship, setting, date, are treated summarily. His approach is professedly preterist-futurist.

Wilcock, Michael (1975), *The Message of Revelation: I Saw Heaven Opened*, The Bible Speaks Today (Downers Grove, Illinois: Inter-Varsity Press).

Wilcock's commentary is very down to earth, written in an engaging style. The units of the book are treated as scenes in a drama. His comments deal with units more than individual verses. A group study guide is included at the end of the book.

Perkins, Pheme (1983), *The Book of Revelation*, Collegeville Bible Commentary (Collegeville, Minnesota: The Liturgical Press).

Perkins' commentary offers a short introduction dealing with genre, authorship, structure, etc. This is followed by an explication of the text based on textual units rather than individual verses. Pictures of Patmos, Ephesus, Pergamum and Smyrna add enjoyment to the clarity of the exposition. Review aids and discussion topics conclude the book.

Morris, Leon (1987), *Revelation* revised ed, Tyndale New Testament Commentaries (Grand Rapids, Michigan: Eerdmans).

This commentary is easy to use. It possesses a short introductory section followed by a straight unit by unit, verse by verse explication of the text. This edition is a revision of his 1969 work.

Metzger, Bruce M. (1993), *Breaking the Code: Understanding the Book of Revelation* (Nashville: Abingdon Press).

Metzger's book was aimed directly at the general readership, focusing on the spiritual message of the book as well as its literary features. The book is very accessible and reads more like a running commentary on large units of text rather than a systematic, detailed analysis. A video and leader's guide are available to complement the use of this commentary.

Talbert, Charles H. (1994), *The Apocalypse: A Reading of the Apocalypse of John* (Louisville, Kentucky: Westminster John Knox Press).

Talbert's book includes a good introductory section which addresses the history of the reception and interpretation of Revelation, in addition to the questions of genre, authorship, purpose and date. The commentary itself is based mostly on units of text which at times become quite small, as witnessed in the individual treatment of each seal, trumpet and bowl. An interesting section on the relevance of Revelation for today's Church concludes the book. Useful end notes allow the reader to go further if desired.

Chapman, Charles T. Jr. (1995), *The Message of the Book of Revelation* (Collegeville, Minnesota: The Liturgical Press).

Chapman's book was aimed intentionally at the general readership. The discussion of alternative interpretations of the symbols are usually avoided. A short section deals with the standard introductory matters. This commentary is performed on a verse-by-verse basis. Each section concludes with a segment called 'Thinking Aloud' where the author addresses the contemporary application of each specific section. The commentaries of R. H. Charles and G. B. Caird form the backbone of Chapman's analysis.

Richard, Pablo (1995), *Apocalypse: A People's Commentary on the Book of Revelation* (Maryknoll, New York: Orbis Books).

Richard, a Chilean priest, is a liberation theologian who is very straightforward as to the hermeneutical principles guiding his interpretation. His introductory section is very well developed and includes elements not found in other books of the same level, especially his tracing of the historical development and other aspects of apocalyptic. Sections of Revelation which he considers to be interrelated are treated together. Each major section is introduced by a presentation of its structure.

González, Catherine Gunsalus and González, Justo L. (1997), *Revelation*, The Westminster Bible Companion (Louisville, Kentucky: Westminster John Knox Press).

Solid, easy to understand basic interpretation of the book of Revelation. The commentary concentrates on units of text instead of individual verses.

### Intermediate

Caird, G. B. (1966), *The Revelation of Saint John*, Black's New Testament Commentary (London: A & C Black/Peabody, Massachusetts: Hendrickson Publishers).

This work is a classic in the world of Revelation studies. The limited number of footnotes makes this an easy-to-read commentary. The treatment is of individual verses with attention being paid to specific words or expressions. Introductory matters are handled summarily, which is surprising for a commentary of this level.

Boring, Eugene M. (1989), *Revelation*, Interpretation: A Bible Commentary for Teaching and Preaching (Louisville: John Knox Press).

Boring's commentary offers an extensive introductory section which develops ten theses concerning topics as diverse as the place of Revelation in the canon, its role as a pastoral letter, audience, authorship, genre, types of interpretation, nature and function of symbolic language, etc. The book addresses units of text rather than individual verses. Four sections called 'Reflection' address specific topics of Revelation.

Krodel, Gerhard A. (1989), *Revelation*, Augsburg Commentary on the New Testament (Minneapolis, Minnesota: Augsburg Publishing House).

This commentary offers an excellent introductory section, especially in its extensive presentation of the history of interpretation of Revelation and millennialism, the context of Revelation, the question of authorship, and the genre of Revelation as a prophetic-apocalyptic circular letter. The setup of the body of the commentary greatly resembles that of Caird's where the words and expressions being explicated are highlighted in bold type. The absence of footnotes and endnotes seems to suggest that Krodel did not want to enter into a dialogue with competing interpretations. The selected bibliography is excellent.

Wall, Robert W. (1991), *Revelation*, New International Biblical Commentary (Peabody, Massachusetts: Hendrickson Publishers).

Wall's commentary is well structured and takes into account much of the work done on Revelation up to the time of his own writing. He discusses the various introductory matters under the banner of four moments in Revelation's history: the moment of origin (date, authorship, audience), the moment of composition (apocalyptic literature, prophecy, letter format), the moment of canonization (history of reception), and the moment of interpretation (five models of interpretation). Wall's additional notes, found at the end of each section, allow him to cover some topics in greater detail and dialogue with the work of other interpreters.

Schüssler Fiorenza, Elisabeth (1991), *Revelation: Vision of a Just World*, Proclamation Commentaries (Minneapolis: Fortress Press).

This commentary was the second produced by Schüssler Fiorenza. Her first work was published in 1985 by Fortress Press and was entitled *The Book of Revelation: Justice and Judgment*. Her 1991 work was still deeply marked by her eclectic approach which combined rhetorical analysis with liberation and feminist biblical criticism. The analysis focused on textual units. Her introductory segment, which defines her approach, as well as the third section, on theo-ethical rhetoric, might prove the most challenging to the reader.

Harrington, Wilfrid J. (1993), *Revelation*, Sacra Pagina (Collegeville, Minnesota: The Liturgical Press).

Harrington's work is a solid intermediate commentary due in part to its format more than to the extent on the interpretation offered. His introduction is thorough, putting due emphasis on the outline of the book as well as its theological perspectives. The suggestions for further study found after the introduction and at the end of each section are excellent. Each segment of the book is divided in three parts: text (his translation), notes (dealing with specific words or expressions in the section being studied, and interpretation (done at a more general level, addressing the passage as a whole). This is done very much in the format of more advanced commentaries. It is this structure which makes it more of an intermediate work rather than an introductory one.

Roloff, Jürgen (1993), *Revelation*, A Continental Commentary (Minneapolis: Fortress Press).

Roloff's work is based on a 'history of influence' approach and great attention is paid to the epistolary format of Revelation. The introduction to the book is standard. Each section of the book is structured as: text, form study or analysis of the passage, and verse-by-verse commentary.

Rowland, Christopher (1993), *Revelation*, Epworth Commentaries (London: Epworth Press).

Rowland's commentary stands out among others due to its original approach. Instead of going for the detailed analysis, Rowland takes on major themes and deals with full chapters instead of individual verses. The value of this commentary lies in the importance paid to the contemporary relevance and meaning of John's Apocalypse. The modern illustrations included alongside his exposition are witness to the evocative power of Revelation's imagery. His introductory section differs from the standard ones by paying a great deal of attention to the interaction between text and reader. Using this work will pay dividends if the student is already familiar with Revelation's text and the interpretations offered by more traditional commentaries.

Court, John M. (1994), *Revelation*, New Testament Guides (Sheffield: Sheffield Academic Press).

As with Rowland's commentary, Court's work will bear its best fruit if used by a reader who has had exposure to traditional commentaries. His approach is very much literary and thematic. His analysis of Revelation's themes is followed by a literary analysis of the book, a study of its social and historical setting, as well as a valuable contribution to the study of Revelation's theology.

Johnson, Alan F. (1996), *Revelation*, The Expositor's Bible Commentary (Grand Rapids, Michigan: Zondervan Publishing House).

Johnson's work contains a standard introduction followed by a short bibliography attempting to categorize well-known commentaries within the four main historical approaches. The body of the commentary is divided into textual units, followed by a verse-by-verse analysis. Each unit is made up of text, exposition and notes. The notes deal with specific textual questions or present interactions with the work of other interpreters, as well as offering suggestions for further study. A solid analysis from a respected scholar.

Garrow, A. J. P. (1997), *Revelation*, New Testament Readings (New York: Routledge).

Garrow tackles the book of Revelation from a consciously literary, narrative approach. His work interacts with well-known studies on Revelation. His emphasis lies on the presence of a story within Revelation. His approach concentrates on the analysis of Revelation's narrative structure, characters, plot and sub-plots. He ingeniously summarized the story of Revelation by using a series of diagrams.

Barr, David L. (1998), *Tales of the End: A Narrative Commentary on the Book of Revelation* (Santa Rosa, California: Polebridge Press).

As the title states, this writer used a full narrative methodology in the study of Revelation. The analysis itself is original and questions many traditional views on the structure of the book. The 'reader's notes' found at the beginning of each section make the reading and use of the book an enjoyable one. The prologue supplies basic narrative theory which later on is very useful in following Barr's argumentation. Many of the topics usually found in the introductory part of most commentaries are contained within the epilogue. This work marks a defining moment in the narrative analysis of the book of Revelation.

Thompson, Leonard L. (1998), *Revelation*, Abingdon New Testament Commentaries (Nashville: Abingdon Press).

Thompson is well known for his *The Book of Revelation: Apocalypse and Empire* (Oxford: Oxford University Press, 1990). The present work is a full-blown commentary, very much the tributary of Thompson's extensive work on Revelation. The analysis deals with individual verses or pairs of verses. His exposition is usually thorough and often refers to ancient Greco-Roman works, Jewish texts and early Christian documents. This commentary should be considered required reading before moving on to the advanced level of study.

### Advanced

*Nota Bene:* The use of the following commentaries generally entails that the reader possesses at least a working knowledge of New Testament Greek and Biblical Hebrew.

Charles, R. H. (1920), *A Critical and Exegetical Commentary on The Revelation of St. John, I and II*, The International Critical Commentary (Edinburgh: T&T Clark).

A classic critical commentary on Revelation, the heir to source- and textual-criticism approaches. This two-volume work represents a foundational moment in the history of Revelation studies. The weakness of Charles' analysis resides in his dissection and reconstruction of the text of Revelation according to his belief in the presence of a later editor. Very few commentators use his reconstruction any more. Charles' extensive study of the grammar of Revelation was a breakthrough in Revelation studies. His attention to detail and thoroughness was quite remarkable. This work remains a must for every serious student of Revelation.

Massyngberde Ford, Josephine (1975), *Revelation*, The Anchor Bible (New York: Doubleday).

Ford's commentary has become famous for the eclectic views adopted throughout the analysis. Her source-critical assessment presented Revelation as including a Jewish apocalypse going back to the Baptist and his circle, a second document written by disciples of the Baptist who might have converted to Christianity, and additional redactional activity conducted by a Jewish Christian, ex-disciple of the Baptist. Her attention to the Jewish sources that might have influenced Revelation make this work a valuable one, even if most interpreters disregard her analysis of the original sources lying behind the final text of Revelation. Ford is in the process of revising her commentary and has abandoned her Baptist hypothesis.

Thomas, Robert L. (1992), *Revelation 1–7: An Exegetical Commentary* (Chicago: Moody Press).
Thomas, Robert L. (1995), *Revelation 8–22: An Exegetical Commentary* (Chicago: Moody Press).

Thomas's work is thorough and represents the best that premillennial/futurist interpretation has to offer. Thorough study is done of specific introductory matters such as the Johannine authorship of Revelation. The analysis is based on the Greek text and addresses each verse. Five excursus are included, the most thought-provoking of which addresses the structure of the Apocalypse: recapitulation or progression. Thomas' conviction of the nature of Revelation's message as predictive prophecy drives his analysis.

Mounce, Robert H. (1998), *The Book of Revelation*, revised ed, The New International Commentary on the New Testament (Grand Rapids, Michigan: Eerdmans).

This work is a revision of Mounce's 1977 commentary which is often considered to be the best evangelical work on Revelation. The format is that of the classical commentary. Even if it does not use the Greek text as much as other advanced commentaries, the analysis is solid and interacts fully with the extensive work that has been done on Revelation in the past twenty years, and even back to the time of R. H. Charles. This would be a great volume to start one's advanced study of Revelation.

Aune, David E. (1997), *Revelation 1–5*, Word Biblical Commentary (Dallas, Texas: Word Publishers).
Aune, David E. (1998), *Revelation 6–16*, Word Biblical Commentary (Nashville: Thomas Nelson Publishers).
Aune, David E. (1998), *Revelation 17–22*, Word Biblical Commentary (Nashville: Thomas Nelson Publishers).

Aune's massive three-volume commentary is the crowning jewel of his extensive work on Revelation. The introduction alone takes 211 pages, covering in great detail the usual introductory topics such as authorship, date, genre and literary structure, as well as more specialized subjects, including source-criticism, text, syntax and vocabulary. Aune's basic thesis, reminiscent of older commentaries, is that Revelation went through two major editions before ending up in the form we possess today. His detailed analysis of sources sometimes overshadows the interpretation of the text itself. The text is dissected with a fine exegetical scalpel but the gathering of the pieces back into a meaningful whole is at times lacking. This work is destined, however, to become a staple of Revelation scholarship.

Beale, Gregory K. (1999), *The Book of Revelation*, The New International Greek Testament Commentary (Grand Rapids, Michigan: Eerdmans/Carlisle: The Paternoster Press).

It seems that Beale was in competition with Aune as to who would provide chiropractors with the greatest number of clients. Beale's 1157-page mammoth commentary, excluding bibliography and indexes, does not come second to anyone. The massive introduction offers his views on topics such as the interpretation of symbols, the use of the Old Testament in Revelation, the significance of 1.19 as interpretive key, the grammar of the Apocalypse, as well as more traditional introductory topics. The analysis found within the body of the commentary is extremely detailed and interacts directly with an extremely wide array of works. The difference of opinion often noticed between Beale and Aune gives the reader a chance to compare detailed analyses of specific passages. This work, alongside Aune's, will surely become foundational for Revelation studies in the next century and beyond.

## Specialized studies

Yarbro Collins, Adela (1976), *The Combat Myth in the Book of Revelation* (Missoula, Montana: Scholars Press).

One of her first important contributions to the study of Revelation. Her analysis of the structure of the book is still very influential today.

Moyise, Steve (1995), *The Old Testament in the Book of Revelation*,

Journal for the Study of the New Testament Supplement Series (Sheffield: Sheffield Academic Press).

A cogently argued presentation of John's use of Old Testament Scriptures in Revelation, mainly Daniel and Ezekiel. The use of Scriptures at Qumran is also treated as well as an enlightening presentation of intertextuality theory and application for Revelation studies.

Bauckham, Richard (1993), *The Climax of Prophecy: Studies on the Book of Revelation* (Edinburgh: T&T Clark).

A very important resource for advanced study of specific topics relating to Revelation: structure and composition, the worship of Jesus in Revelation, the role of the Spirit, etc. A must for every serious student of Revelation.

Bauckham, Richard (1993), *The Theology of the Book of Revelation*, New Testament Theology (Cambridge: Cambridge University Press).

One of the few book-length treatments of the theology found in Revelation. Some of the topics covered in this book are analysed in greater detail in his *The Climax of Prophecy*. This work can be of use for all levels of study.

## Summary

The book of Revelation stands before the reader as an invitation to discovery. Whether for spiritual or academic purposes, individual or communal, the strangeness and vividness of its images beckon the reader to enter its world and unravel the tapestry of meaning it holds within its pages. On accepting this invitation, the student of Revelation must decide where to start and how to undertake this task. This chapter was intended to offer some non-exhaustive guidelines and resources to allow any one to benefit from an interaction with the writing of John the seer. The book's complexity and beauty is sure to captivate the readers and keep them coming back for more.

As for anything this complex, it is wise to rely on the experience of people who have been there before. Commentaries and articles on Revelation abound. Each usually holds at least one insight which can be assimilated into one's own encounter with the Apocalypse of John. The warning to heed is to refrain from relying on only one specific commentary, even monumental works like those of Aune and Beale, while conducting a study of the book of Revelation: 'Start with one, but do not stop at one.' Comparison becomes the main tool in order to assess the value of every writer's individual interpretation. Revelation's complexity will always be too much for a single commentator. Certain points are downplayed by some, while highlighted by others. The use of varied sources should remedy these vagaries of the exegetical task. Most of all, the reader should make this a valuable, enjoyable experience. Revelation is comfort, encouragement, and warning addressed to those concerned with the presence of God in a world which seems determined to deny his existence. The study of Revelation should therefore remain primarily a transforming experience, even when practised at the highest level of academia. As St Augustine heard the little voice say: '*Tolle et lege*', 'take and read'.

# 8

## Conclusion: The future of Revelation

### Recovering Revelation as a Christian book speaking to the churches today

The arrival of the new millennium has sparked various reactions, fears and expectations throughout the world. Some of these came true, others not. In all of this, the book of Revelation has sometimes become an unwilling participant. Fear mongers and cultic conventicles have tried as much they could to spread their existential anguish to the majority of the population, with often a very restricted amount of success. The world is still turning and all are trying to cope with their New Year's resolutions.

Out of this, Christianity must now make good on its responsibility to rescue the book of Revelation from the grips of fanatics and sectarians, and bring it back within the fold of the Christian message. The end-of-days expectations are fast losing their appeal and many doomsayers will need to update their edition of *The Late Great Planet Earth*, or the prophecies of Nostradamus. Christians, however, should seize this opportunity to reconcile themselves with the book of Revelation. As we have observed throughout this introduction, Revelation is not basically a blueprint of the end of the world or just an antiquated archive. It remains alive with possibilities. It beckons one to feed on its images and encounter the Living Christ who still today stands in the midst of his churches, encouraging, comforting and exhorting. Without practicing any kind of illegitimate transfer of meaning, it is possible, as we have seen in chapter 6, to compare some of the situations portrayed in Revelation to our contemporary setting. The Roman Empire, with its claims to divinity and sole object of worship, is still alive today. The beast is constantly lurking around. Christians still face challenges to their faith, having to interact with a culture which is basically neo-pagan, offering various types of idols to worship. This new century and new millennium are replete with fresh and exciting possibilities to encounter, and be transformed, by the message of Revelation. If humanity is to change for the better, Christians will have to strive to fulfil the will of the One seated on the throne who makes everything new (Rev 21.5).

## Apocalypse now: Revelation and the doomsday mentality

Throughout its history, the book of Revelation has been constantly linked to a phenomenon known as apocalyptic. This mentality was born, in its literary form, at the time of the prophet Zoroaster. It reached its pinnacle of expression in the period between the revolt of the Maccabees (165 BCE) and the writing of the Book of Revelation (second half of first century CE). The apocalyptic mentality however survived, becoming the source of numerous doomsday scenarios and predictions of the end of the world. It has manifested itself in a very public way through the suicide of several groups who held to such a mindset. At the beginning of this new century, the authorities, going from the FBI, Scotland Yard, and the Israeli Mossad, are not so much concerned about the end of the world happening as to groups deciding to make it happen. From Berlin to Georgia to Calgary, well-armed doomsday cults are ready to make the Apocalypse happen, if it does not on its own. This is the scariest manifestation of the doomsday mentality.

Our contemporary world has also transformed and updated the way in which the apocalyptic/doomsday mentality is transmitted. Books and movies have become the favourite means of expressing the world's apocalyptic fears. Very often, the book of Revelation becomes linked to these fears. Its images are then misinterpreted and misused by many to express their conviction that this world is coming to an end. Well-known apocalyptic feature films which borrowed ideas and concepts from Revelation include *The Omen*, *The Seventh Sign*, *The Prophecy*, *Armageddon* and *End of Days*. Human fascination with the end of all things seems to be insatiable.

Apocalyptic, however, is more than just end-of-the-world talk. It is hope and knowledge that good, in the end, will prevail over evil; that there is something better awaiting humanity; that our individual and corporate lives hold eternal value in the grand scheme of things. The present is not all that there is, things are not always what they seem to be. The book of Revelation carries such apocalyptic hope. The Lord of Creation is also the Lord of History. In anyone's darkest hour, his Christ stands at the door knocking, awaiting to be let inside (Rev 3.20). Hollywood's special effects might influence an enthralled audience for two hours, but the apocalyptic message of Revelation transcends time.

# Bibliography

Aichele, George and Phillips, Gary A. (1995), 'Introduction: Exegesis, Eisegesis, Intergesis, Intertextuality and the Bible', *Semeia*, 69–70, 7–18.

Alford, Henry (1958), 'Apocalypse of John', *The Greek Testament* Vol. 4 (Chicago: Moody).

Arens Kuckerlkorn, Eduardo, Díaz Mateos, Manuel and Kraft, Tomás (1998), 'Revelation', in William R. Farmer (ed.), *The International Bible Commentary* (Collegeville, Minnesota: The Liturgical Press).

Aune, David E. (1997), *Revelation 1–5*, Word Biblical Commentary (Dallas, Texas: Word Publishers).

Aune, David E. (1998a), *Revelation 17–22*, Word Biblical Commentary (Nashville: Thomas Nelson Publishers).

Aune, David E. (1998b), *Revelation 6–16*, Word Biblical Commentary (Nashville: Thomas Nelson Publishers).

Barr, David L. (1998), *Tales of the End: A Narrative Commentary on the Book of Revelation* (Santa Rosa, California: Polebridge Press).

Bauckham, Richard (1993a), *The Climax of Prophecy: Studies on the Book of Revelation* (Edinburgh: T&T Clark).

Bauckham, Richard (1993b), *The Theology of the Book of Revelation*, New Testament Theology (Cambridge: Cambridge University Press).

Beale, Gregory K. (1999), *The Book of Revelation*, The New International Greek Testament Commentary (Grand Rapids, Michigan: Eerdmans/Carlisle: The Paternoster Press).

Boesak, Allan A. (1987), *Comfort and Protest: The Apocalypse from a South African Perspective* (Philadelphia: Westminster).

Boring, Eugene M. (1989), *Revelation*. (Series: Interpretation: A Bible Commentary for Teaching and Preaching (Louisville: John Knox Press).

Bousset, Wilhelm (1906), *Die Offenbarung Johannis* (6th edn) (Göttingen: Vandenhoeck und Ruprecht).

Caird, G. B. (1966), *The Revelation of Saint John*, Black's New Testament Commentary (London: A&C Black/Peabody, Massachusetts: Hendrickson Publishers).

Callahan, Allen Dwight (1995), 'The Language of Apocalypse', *Harvard Theological Review* 88, (October), pp. 453–70.

Chapman, Charles T. Jr. (1995), *The Message of the Book of Revelation* (Collegeville, Minnesota: The Liturgical Press).

Charles, R. H. (1920), *A Critical and Exegetical Commentary on The Revelation of St. John, I and II*, The International Critical Commentary (Edinburgh: T&T Clark).

Collins, John J. (1979), 'Introduction: Toward the Morphology of a Genre', *Semeia* 14, 1–20.

Cook, Stephen L. (1995), 'Reflections on Apocalypticism at the Approach of the Year 2000', *Union Seminary Quarterly Review* 1–4, 1–16.

Court, John M. (1994), *Revelation*, New Testament Guides (Sheffield: Sheffield Academic Press).

Deissmann, Adolph (1965), *Light from the Ancient East*, New Edition, trans. L. R. M. Strachan (Grand Rapids, Michigan: Baker).

Eco, Umberto and Martini, Carlo Maria (1997), 'Hope for the New Millennium: An Exchange between Umberto Eco and Carlo Maria Martini', *Cross Currents* (Fall 1997), 379–87.

Garrow, A. J. P. (1997), *Revelation*, New Testament Readings (New York: Routledge).

Genette, Gérard (1980), *Narrative Discourse: An Essay in Method*, trans. Jane E. Lewin (New York: Cornell University Press).

Gentry, Kenneth L. Jr. (1998), 'A Preterist View of Revelation' in C. Marvin Pate (ed.), *Four Views on the Book of Revelation* (Grand Rapids, Michigan: Zondervan Publishing House).

González, Catherine Gunsalus and González, Justo L. (1997), *Revelation*, The Westminster Bible Companion (Louisville, Kentucky: Westminster John Knox Press).

Grenz, Stanley J. and Olson, Roger E. (1992), *Twentieth Century Theology: God and the World in a Transitional Age* (Illinois: Intervarsity Press).

Harrington, Wilfrid J. (1993), *Revelation*, Sacra Pagina (Collegeville, Minnesota: The Liturgical Press).

Hendricksen, William (1944), *More than Conquerors* (Grand Rapids, Michigan: Baker).

Johnson, Alan F. (1996), *Revelation*, The Expositor's Bible Commentary (Grand Rapids, Michigan: Zondervan Publishing House).

Keller, Catherine (1996), *Apocalypse Now and Then* (Boston: Beacon Press).

Knight, Jonathan (1999), *Revelation* (Sheffield: Sheffield Academic Press).

Kristeva, Julia (1969), *Semiotiké: Recherches pour une Sémanalyse* (Paris: Le Seuil).

Krodel, Gerhard A. (1989), *Revelation*, Augsburg Commentary on the New Testament (Minneapolis, Minnesota: Augsburg Publishing House).

Ladd, George Eldon (1972), *A Commentary on the Revelation of John* (Grand Rapids, Michigan: Eerdmans).

Lindsey, Hal (1970), *The Late Great Planet Earth* (New York: Bantam Books).

Malina, Bruce J. (1995), *On the Genre and Message of Revelation: Star Visions and Sky Journeys* (Massachusetts: Hendricksen Publishers).

Massyngberde Ford, Josephine (1975), *Revelation*, The Anchor Bible (New York: Doubleday).

Metzger, Bruce M. (1993), *Breaking the Code: Understanding the Book of Revelation* (Nashville: Abingdon Press).

Morris, Leon (1987), *Revelation*, revised edn Tyndale New Testament Commentaries (Grand Rapids, Michigan: Eerdmans.

Mounce, Robert H. (1998), *The Book of Revelation*, revised edn The New International Commentary on the New Testament (Grand Rapids, Michigan: Eerdmans).

Moyise, Steve (1995), *The Old Testament in the Book of Revelation*, Journal for the Study of the New Testament Supplement Series (Sheffield: Sheffield Academic Press).

Moyise, Steve (1998), *Introduction to Biblical Studies* (London: Cassell).

Noble, Paul R. (1993), 'Synchronic and Diachronic Approaches to Biblical Interpretation', *Literature and Theology*, Vol. VII, no 2, (June), 130–48.

Perkins, Pheme (1983), *The Book of Revelation*, Collegeville Bible Commentary (Collegeville, Minnesota: The Liturgical Press).

Pippin, Tina (1992), *Death and Desire: The Rhetoric of Gender in the Apocalypse of John* (Louisville: Westminster/John Knox Press).

Pippin, Tina (1999), *Apocalyptic Bodies: The Biblical End of the World in Text and Image* (New York: Routledge).

Prévost, Jean-Pierre (1983), *Pour en Finir avec la Peur: L'Apocalypse* (Montréal: Les Editions Paulines).

Powell, Mark Allan (1990), *What Is Narrative Criticism?*, Guides to Biblical Scholarship, ed. Dan O. Via Jr. (Minneapolis: Fortress Press).

Richard, Pablo (1995), *Apocalypse: A People's Commentary on the Book of Revelation* (Maryknoll, New York: Orbis Books).

Roloff, Jürgen (1993), *Revelation*, A Continental Commentary (Minneapolis: Fortress Press).

Rowland, Christopher (1993), *Revelation*, Epworth Commentaries (London: Epworth Press).

Ryken, Leland (1992), *Words of Delight: A Literary Introduction to the Bible*, 2nd edn (Grand Rapids, Michigan: Baker Book House).

Schüssler Fiorenza, Elisabeth (1991), *Revelation: Vision of a Just World*, Proclamation Commentaries (Minneapolis: Fortress Press).

Scofield, Cyrus I. (1909), *The Scofield Reference Bible* (Oxford: Oxford University Press).

Smalley, Stephen S. (1987), 'John's Revelation and John's Community', *Bulletin of the John Rylands Library* 69 (Spring), 549–71.

Stoutzenberger, Joseph (1993), *Celebrating Sacraments* (Winona, Minnesota: Saint Mary's Press).

Swete, Henry B. (1906), *The Apocalypse of St. John* (London: Macmillan).

Talbert, Charles H. (1994), *The Apocalypse: A Reading of the Apocalypse of John* (Louisville, Kentucky: Westminster John Knox Press).

Thomas, Robert L. (1992), *Revelation 1–7: An Exegetical Commentary* (Chicago: Moody Press).

Thomas, Robert L. (1995), *Revelation 8–22: An Exegetical Commentary* (Chicago: Moody Press).

Thompson, Leonard L. (1998), *Revelation*, Abingdon New Testament Commentaries (Nashville: Abingdon Press).

Tyrrell, George (1909), *Christianity at the Cross-Roads* (London: George Allen & Unwin).

Wall, Robert W. (1991), *Revelation*, New International Biblical Commentary (Peabody, Massachusetts: Hendrickson Publishers).

Wilcock, Michael (1975), *The Message of Revelation: I Saw Heaven Opened*, The Bible Speaks Today (Downers Grove, Illinois: Inter-Varsity Press).

World Council of Churches (1980), *The Bible: Its Authority and Interpretation in the Ecumenical Movement*, Faith and Order Paper No. 99 (Geneva, Switzerland: WCC).

Yarbro Collins, Adela (1976), *The Combat Myth in the Book of Revelation* (Missoula, Montana: Scholars Press).

Yarbro Collins, Adela (1986), 'Introduction: Early Christian Apocalypticism' in Adela Yarbro Collins (ed.), *Early Christian Apocalypticism: Genre and Social Setting Semeia 36* (Decatur, Georgia: Scholars Press).

Yarbro Collins, Adela (1998), 'The Book of Revelation' in John J. Collins (ed.), *The Encyclopedia of Apocalypticism, Vol. I The Origins of Apocalypticism in Judaism and Christianity* (New York: Continuum).

# Index of Modern Authors

# General Index